To

_____

From

_____

Date

_____

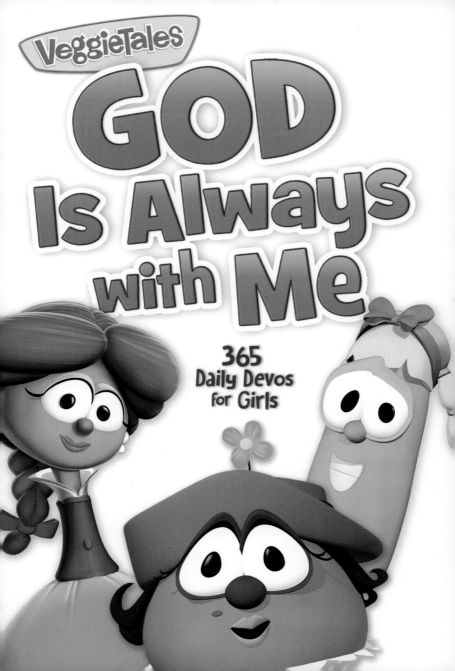

VeggieTales

GOD
Is Always
with Me

365
Daily Devos
for Girls

veggietales.com

ISBN: 978-1-5460-1397-6 (paperback)
ISBN: 978-1-5460-0060-0 (padded hardcover)

WorthyKids
Hachette Book Group
1290 Avenue of the Americas, New York, NY 10104

WorthyKids is a division of Hachette Book Group, Inc. The WorthyKids name and logo are trademarks of Hachette Book Group, Inc.

Printed and bound in China
APS
10 9 8 7 6 5 4 3 2 1

VeggieTales

GOD
Is Always
with Me

365
Daily Devos
for Girls

A NOTE TO PARENTS OR GRANDPARENTS

As a parent or grandparent, you know the importance of teaching children the big ideas that are found in God's Word and encouraging them to spend time with Him. The daily devotions in this book will help you do that.

Each entry contains a Bible verse and a kid-friendly devotion on an important topic such as honesty, forgiveness, or kindness. A question or thought follows to reinforce the message for the day, and a daily prayer will help your child to develop a habit of talking to God.

During the coming year, encourage your daughter or granddaughter to read a devotion from this book every day. This will help her establish a daily practice of hearing from God. It will also provide 365 opportunities to share God's love and wisdom and a daily chance for her to be reminded that God made her special—He knows her so well and loves her very much.

BE A BLESSING

"It is more blessed to give than to receive."

ACTS 20:35B ESV

The word "blessed" means to be happy. Jesus says we will be happier giving to others than just getting things for ourselves. When you take time to think about what will make someone else happy, you will feel happier too!

You may not have money to spend on fancy gifts, but you can always give a hug, share a smile, lend a toy to a friend, draw a picture, or make a card. As you think about giving something to others, you will start to feel happy, and probably even excited! Be a blessing, and you will be blessed!

THOUGHT OF THE DAY

What is one way you can be a blessing to someone in your family?

PRAY TODAY

Dear God, thank You for all You give to me every single day. Please help me find ways to be a blessing to others. Amen.

SHARING BRINGS JOY

Do not neglect to do good and to share what you have, for such sacrifices are pleasing to God.

HEBREWS 13:16 ESV

God has given you many wonderful things—a smile, great ideas, books, toys, adventures, flowers, and lots more! Do you know why God gives His children so much? It's so that we have things to share with each other.

God made us, so He knows that we are happiest when we give some of what we have to other people. You can share a smile with a sad friend, read a story to someone, sing a song, paint a picture, or share a toy. When you share, you make God happy, and you are happier too! That's real joy.

THOUGHT OF THE DAY

Think about something you can share with someone . . . then do it!

PRAY TODAY

Dear God, thank You for giving me so much. Help me bring joy to others by sharing what I have with them. Amen.

CREATIVE KINDNESS

Finally, all of you, be like-minded, be sympathetic, love one another, be compassionate and humble.

1 PETER 3:8 NIV

God gave you a wonderful creative mind. You can use your imagination to make-believe with your friends or draw beautiful pictures. And guess how else you can practice creativity? Being kind!

Look for nice things you can do for the people around you. Can you pick up trash that someone left at the park? Rake your neighbor's leaves? Make up a silly song to cheer up a friend? Help your parents make dinner? There are so many ways to be kind. Ask God to show you a new way today!

THOUGHT OF THE DAY

How did someone show you kindness today?

PRAY TODAY

Dear God, thank You for my imagination! Please help me think of new ways to be kind every day. Amen.

BRING THE LIGHT

The light shines in the darkness, and the darkness has not overcome it.

JOHN 1:5 ESV

When you go into a dark room and turn on the light, what happens? The darkness goes away! When the sun comes up, what happens to the dark night? It goes away!

When Jesus lives in you, you are like a light, shining in the darkness. How does that work? If someone is sad, and you offer them kindness, you're sharing the light of Jesus. If someone tells a lie, and you say what is true, your words help everyone see what's right. When you belong to Jesus, you carry His light wherever you go. And God's light always chases away the darkness.

THOUGHT OF THE DAY

How can you bring Jesus' light to someone today?

PRAY TODAY

Dear God, help me look for ways to bring Your light to others today. Amen.

@ @ @ @ @ @ @

DO SOMETHING BIG!

You are young, but do not let anyone treat you as if you were not important. Be an example to show the believers how they should live. Show them with your words, with the way you live, with your love, with your faith, and with your pure life.

1 TIMOTHY 4:12 ICB

Has someone ever told you that you're too little to do something? That's frustrating, isn't it? But even though there are some things only grown-ups or older kids can do, you can do some really big things too! When you invite a new friend to play, you help him or her feel loved and important. When you share what you have, you show God's love. And when you pray, you're talking to the King of the whole universe! The things you do matter big-time to God.

THOUGHT OF THE DAY

With God's help, little people can do great big things!

PRAY TODAY

Dear God, sometimes it's hard to be little. Please show me what kinds of big things I can do for You! Amen.

TALKING TO GOD

I cried to him for help; I praised him with songs.

PSALM 66:17 GNT

Do you have a good friend you love talking to? Friends share joys and even sadness with each other. God is a friend who wants to hear all about what is going on in your life too!

Talking to God is called prayer. And you can pray anytime you want to. God is always around! You can tell Him when you're feeling sad or even mad. You can talk about happy times and scary times. When you pray, you can whisper or shout or even sing! God loves to hear your voice.

THOUGHT OF THE DAY

What are some things you want to tell God about right now?

PRAY TODAY

Dear God, thank You for being my best friend. Help me to remember to talk with You every day. Amen.

FRIENDS HELP FRIENDS

You use steel to sharpen steel, and one friend sharpens another.

PROVERBS 27:17 MSG

There are many ways that friends help one another. One way you might not know about is how one friend can "sharpen" another.

When two pieces of steel are rubbed together, they make each other sharp by smoothing out rough edges. Friends sharpen one another when they help the other person make good choices. Sometimes a friend needs to be reminded to be kinder or to try harder. That's not always easy to hear—or say!—but good friends listen and learn from one another. Then they each become better!

THOUGHT OF THE DAY

Friends who help each other grow are the best friends we can know!

PRAY TODAY

Dear God, thanks for giving me good friends who love me and help me grow. Help me to be a good friend too. Amen.

LET'S GET ALONG!

Work at getting along with each other and with God.

HEBREWS 12:14 MSG

It's easy to get along with people who are just like us. But the world is full of people who think and act differently from us. God wants us to work hard to get along with everyone—not just the people we already like.

Start by showing kindness to everyone you meet. Get to know people who are different from you. You probably won't become best friends with each person. And there may be things you disagree about. That's OK! Getting along means appreciating what makes each other special. Then, you can all work together to learn, grow, and do big things.

THOUGHT OF THE DAY

Is there someone who is hard to get along with? How can you show kindness to that person?

PRAY TODAY

Dear God, thank You for making all kinds of people. Help me get along with those who are different from me! Amen.

WONDERFULLY MADE

I will praise You because I have been remarkably and wonderfully made.

PSALM 139:14A HCSB

Have you ever looked at an invention and wondered who made it? How did they decide to put it together? How did they make it work just right? Well, *you* are one of the most amazing creations in the world. Do you know that you have been made by God? He decided just the right way to make you, and He says you are remarkable and wonderful! Even if there are times when you don't feel very special, God says you are! You can trust that God made you exactly the way you should be. He loves you and has great plans for you.

THOUGHT OF THE DAY

You are a wonderful creation, made by God.

PRAY TODAY

Thank You, God, for loving me and making me just the way You wanted me to be. Amen.

HAVE COURAGE

Wait for the LORD; be strong, and let your heart take courage; wait for the LORD!

PSALM 27:14 ESV

The Bible is full of courageous heroes. Queen Esther risked her life to save her people from an evil man. David the shepherd boy fought a giant and won. Gideon led 300 soldiers carrying only horns and lamps, and they defeated an army of 135,000!

You might think that brave people never feel scared. But that's not true! Courage doesn't mean you don't have any fear. You show courage when you do something *even though* you feel afraid because you know God is with you! When you trust God, He will give you courage.

THOUGHT OF THE DAY

When you feel scared, pray and wait for God's courage!

PRAY TODAY

Dear God, please help me to be brave even when I feel afraid. I'm so glad You're always by my side! Amen.

UNCONDITIONAL LOVE

And so we know the love that God has for us, and we trust that love. God is love.

1 JOHN 4:16 ICB

People often use a special word to describe God's love: *unconditional.* That means we don't have to do anything to get His love. It's already there. We don't have to say or do the right thing all the time. We can make mistakes and try again. Nothing will ever make God stop loving us.

God loves you just the way you are, and He loves to spend time with you! So share your thoughts and feelings with God every day. He is full of love and ready to listen to you.

THOUGHT OF THE DAY

God has always loved you, and He always will.

PRAY TODAY

Dear God, thank You for loving me all the time, no matter what! I love You too. Amen.

TRUE FRIENDS

A friend loves you all the time.

PROVERBS 17:17 ICB

What do you and your friends like to do together? Do you make each other laugh? Do you have favorite games? It's important to have fun together, of course! But God says a true friend sticks around even if things aren't always fun.

When your friends have a bad day, make sure they know that you still love them. If you get into an argument, be willing to listen and say "sorry" when you need to. And remember that your friends should love you on your bad days too. When you find true friends, hang on to them!

THOUGHT OF THE DAY

True friends are true gifts from God!

PRAY TODAY

Dear God, thank You for the gift of friends. Please help me find—and be!—a true friend. Amen.

CHOOSE GOD'S WAY

"Do everything the LORD your God requires. Live the way he wants you to. Obey his orders and commands."

1 KINGS 2:3A NIRV

King David gave his son Solomon some very good advice: obey God all the time. King David knew that it's not always easy to do what God says, but it's always the right choice.

We all have to make choices. Should you share or be selfish? Should you say kind words or hurting words? Should you obey your parents or just do whatever you want? Whenever you have to make a choice, stop and think: What would Jesus do? Then do that! God will be happy you listened to Him.

THOUGHT OF THE DAY

You can choose what's right today. Just follow Jesus and obey!

PRAY TODAY

Dear God, help me make choices that make You happy. I want to follow Jesus every day. Amen.

PRACTICE THE TRUTH

We are part of the same body. Stop lying and start telling each other the truth.

EPHESIANS 4:25 CEV

How do you get better at playing an instrument? You practice! In fact, it would be silly to walk into a recital and expect to play well if you hadn't been practicing.

Honesty is the same way. When you practice often, you're always ready to perform! If you aren't used to telling the truth, you can slip into telling big lies. Big lies can hurt feelings and cause trouble. But when you tell the truth all the time—even about small things—it's easier not to lie when big things come along. That's well worth putting in the practice time!

THOUGHT OF THE DAY

Tell the truth, and you will see, each time comes more easily!

PRAY TODAY

Dear God, please help me tell the truth all the time. I want to be someone people can trust! Amen.

@ @ @ @ @ @ @

SLOW YOUR ANGER

Don't let your spirit rush to be angry, for anger abides in the heart of fools.

ECCLESIASTES 7:9 HCSB

There's nothing wrong with feeling angry sometimes. But if you get mad really easily, that's no fun for anyone. Good news: God can help slow down your anger!

For example, imagine you want to play soccer today, but your friend doesn't. That might make you feel angry! But instead of yelling or stomping away, take a breath. What are some ways you both could have fun? Is there something else you love to do together? It takes practice, but God can help you turn a quick temper into quick problem-solving!

THOUGHT OF THE DAY

Don't rush into feeling mad. Find a way you'll all be glad!

PRAY TODAY

Dear God, sometimes I get angry so quickly, I can't stop my words. Please help me slow down. I can do anything with Your help! Amen.

GOD MAKES YOU STRONG

We say they are happy because they did not give up.

JAMES 5:11A NCV

Have you ever done something really hard? It takes a lot of work to learn a new skill or finish a big job or even make new friends! And sometimes you might get tired and feel like giving up.

Hang in there! God can make you strong enough to do anything. Ask for His help and watch what He does. He can give you new ideas and fresh courage. He can even bring along people to help you! Nothing is too hard for God! With Him by your side, you can do anything.

THOUGHT OF THE DAY

What's something that you need to do? Ask God—He loves helping you!

PRAY TODAY

Dear God, sometimes I feel too tired to finish what I started. Please make me strong and help me do great things! Amen.

@ @ @ @ @ @ @ @

GOD'S PERFECT TIMING

"Who knows? Maybe you were made queen for just such a time as this."

ESTHER 4:14 MSG

Queen Esther was very brave. She trusted God and always tried to listen to Him. One day, Esther overheard a plan to hurt her family and the people she loved. She wanted to stop it, but she was afraid she would get hurt too. Her cousin, Mordecai, reminded her that God's plans are perfect. Maybe God had even made her queen for this very moment! Queen Esther spoke up to the king and stopped the evil plans.

God has given you your friends, your family, and your neighborhood for a reason. Look around. Who can you help today?

THOUGHT OF THE DAY

God's plans always happen at the right time—God's time!

PRAY TODAY

Dear God, please help me trust You always. Your plans and timing are perfect! Amen.

LIGHT IS BIGGER THAN DARKNESS

Then Jesus spoke to them again, saying, "I am the light of the world. He who follows Me shall not walk in darkness, but have the light of life."

JOHN 8:12 NKJV

It's hard to see anything in a dark room. But flip on a light switch, and BANG! Suddenly everything is clear!

Things like worry, fear, and confusion act like darkness in our lives. It's hard to see beyond them. But the Bible tells us that Jesus is a light. So following Jesus is like flipping on a giant light switch! We can give Jesus all our worries. We can feel less afraid because He is stronger than everything! He can even help us understand new things when we get confused or lost. Jesus' light makes everything clearer.

THOUGHT OF THE DAY
Every day is brighter with Jesus in it.

PRAY TODAY
Dear God, thank You for sending Jesus to light up the world! Amen.

ASK FOR PEACE

"Peace I leave with you; my peace I give you. I do not give to you as the world gives. Do not let your hearts be troubled and do not be afraid."

JOHN 14:27 NIV

Jesus knows that sometimes we worry or feel afraid. He understands when we are shy or upset. But Jesus also knows how to help when we feel like this: He gives us His peace!

Jesus can make our hearts feel calm when we are worried. His peace helps us feel less afraid. He is always with us and promises to give us peace when we ask Him for it. When you are upset, ask Jesus to fill your heart with His peace and calm. Then trust Him to do it.

THOUGHT OF THE DAY

Can you think of a time when you needed Jesus to fill your heart with peace?

PRAY TODAY

Dear Jesus, thank You for the peace You give me. Help me to remember to ask You for it whenever I worry or feel afraid. Amen.

USE YOUR GIFTS

God has given each of you a gift from his great variety of spiritual gifts. Use them well to serve one another.

1 PETER 4:10 NLT

You are a wonderful, special creation! God made you different from anyone else on Earth. He gave you your smile, your laugh, your likes, and even your dislikes. And He also gave you spiritual gifts!

Spiritual gifts are special abilities God gave you to use for Him. Maybe you are a terrific listener, and others feel comforted when they talk with you. Maybe you like to read Scripture in church. Do you like to share Jesus' story with your friends? Or sing in a choir? Ask God to show you what gifts He's given you. Then use them to praise God— and help others!

THOUGHT OF THE DAY

There is only one you! How do you love to praise God and serve people?

PRAY TODAY

Dear God, please show me the ways You've made me special. I want to use my gifts well! Amen.

A SPECIAL PROMISE

"Honor your father and mother. Then you will live a long, full life in the land the LORD your God is giving you."

EXODUS 20:12 NLT

God gave some special rules to Moses. We call them the Ten Commandments. One of these commandments has a special promise attached. Read the verse above, and see if you can tell what it is.

The promise says that if you honor your father and mother, then God will bless you with a good life. But what does it mean to honor your parents? It means to show them respect, listen to them, and do what they say. It also means to show them love and kindness. When you do these things, your life is better and your family is happier too!

THOUGHT OF THE DAY

What are some ways you can honor your mom and dad today?

PRAY TODAY

Dear God, thank You for my parents. Please show me how I can honor them every day. Amen.

GOD'S VIP

Do not be lazy but work hard, serving the Lord with all your heart.

ROMANS 12:11 NCV

Someone who is rich and famous is sometimes called a VIP—a Very Important Person. But Jesus says that the most important people are those who serve others. That means anyone can be God's VIP!

Serving someone can look like all kinds of things. You could make a card for a sick neighbor or offer to take your friend's dog for a walk. Maybe a younger friend or sibling is learning something new. Can you help? Look for ways to help all the people in your life. God needs you to be His VIP!

THOUGHT OF THE DAY

When you work hard to serve someone else, God blesses both of you.

PRAY TODAY

Dear Jesus, I want to be Your VIP. Please show me how I can serve the people around me, and help me work hard! Amen.

GOOD INGREDIENTS

"A good man brings good things out of the good stored up in him."

MATTHEW 12:35A NIV

Have you ever had chocolate chip cookies? Imagine if you put pickles in the batter instead of chocolate chips! Yuck! But when you use the right ingredients, you can't help but make a delicious treat.

It's the same with good deeds. Good deeds are kind actions that are like treats for the heart. And in order to make delicious heart-treats, you need to start with the best ingredient: goodness! Think kindly of others and never spread gossip. Search for good things in everything that happens. Thank God all the time! When goodness fills your heart, you can make a whole batch of good deeds!

THOUGHT OF THE DAY

Stock up on goodness today, so you can serve up good deeds tomorrow!

PRAY TODAY

Dear God, please help me fill my heart with good ingredients, so I can bless others! Amen.

LET'S PARTY!

A cheerful heart has a continual feast.

PROVERBS 15:15 HCSB

Isn't it hard to go home when you're having fun at a party? Well, God says that having a cheerful heart is just like a great party—except you never have to leave!

You can have a cheerful heart by noticing all the gifts God has given you. Not just the things you ask for—like presents on Christmas or pizza day at school. Look at what He gives you every day! There's warm sunshine, bright rainbows, funny friends, a loving family, sparkly stars, and yummy food. When you're praising God, your joy will never end. And neither will the party in your heart!

THOUGHT OF THE DAY
With God, party time is all the time!

PRAY TODAY
Dear God, please give me a cheerful heart so I can always party with You! Amen.

GOD'S LOVE IS FOREVER

But for those who honor the LORD, his love lasts forever, and his goodness endures for all generations.

PSALM 103:17 GNT

Every spring and summer, flowers bloom with bright colors and trees fill with green leaves. Every fall, leaves turn red and orange and brown. Then, winter snow might even cover the ground until spring warms it up again! The world is always changing. And so are you! You are learning new things, making new friends, and even growing out of old clothes! But one thing never changes. God's love is the same today as it was yesterday. It will be the same tomorrow and next week and next year. It will never fade away and you cannot lose it. It's yours forever!

THOUGHT OF THE DAY

The love of God is always there. You'll never lose His tender care.

PRAY TODAY

Dear God, thank You for loving me now and forever. I am so glad I'm Your child. Amen.

FAMILY RESEMBLANCE

So God created human beings in his own image.

GENESIS 1:27A NLT

Sometimes kids look like their parents. Maybe your hair is curly like your mom's, or your eyes are the same color as your dad's. That's called family resemblance. And it happens in God's family too!

The Bible says God made people in His image—so we all look a little like Him! Just like God, we can feel and share love, enjoy beautiful things, and make good choices. And when we treat people kindly and choose to help instead of hurt, others will see God in us! What a great family resemblance!

THOUGHT OF THE DAY

How can you show someone what God looks like today?

PRAY TODAY

Dear God, thank You for creating me to be Your child! I love being in Your family. Amen.

SNEAKY GOODNESS

None of you should look out just for your own good. Each of you should also look out for the good of others.

PHILIPPIANS 2:4 NIRV

Some people get a lot of attention for doing good deeds. But God doesn't care about attention. He wants you to choose kind actions just because you want to help others.

Here's a fun way to do God's kind of goodness. Think of someone who needs to be cheered up. Then make something special for them—you could draw a pretty picture or maybe ask a parent to help you bake a yummy treat! Now leave the gift somewhere they'll find it, but don't tell anyone who it's from. They will feel happier and loved. But only you and God will know about your sneaky goodness!

THOUGHT OF THE DAY

How would you feel if someone gave you a sneaky gift?

PRAY TODAY

Dear God, please show me how to help others every day, even when no one's paying attention! Amen.

THE KEY TO HAPPINESS

Rejoice always! Pray constantly. Give thanks in everything, for this is God's will for you in Christ Jesus.

1 THESSALONIANS 5:16–18 HCSB

God gives us three secrets to a happy life. First, praise God for what He's done. These can be small things, like the way He's made flowers smell so sweet, or big things, like giving you a loving family. Second, pray all the time. That doesn't mean you should walk around with your eyes closed and hands folded! Just talk to God during your day. And third, give thanks no matter what. Even if things don't go your way, look for something to be thankful for anyway. When you follow God's three steps, you'll be surprised how much happiness you'll find!

THOUGHT OF THE DAY

Find a reason to praise God and a reason to thank Him. Then pray and tell Him what you found!

PRAY TODAY

Dear God, there is so much to be glad about! Help me remember to pray, praise, and say thanks every day. Amen.

ⓔ ⓐ ⓔ ⓐ ⓔ ⓔ ⓐ

PROTECTING ANGELS

For he will order his angels to protect you wherever you go.

PSALM 91:11 NLT

Angels are special beings that do special jobs for God. Once, angels brought food to Isaiah, one of God's helpers. When baby Jesus was born, angels told the shepherds where to find Him. In heaven, angels sing songs of praise to God. The Bible tells us about another very important job that angels do—they protect us! Even though you may not see angels around you, you can be sure they are there, helping and protecting you. They are one of the many ways God shows His love for you.

THOUGHT OF THE DAY

All day, all night, angels are watching over you!

PRAY TODAY

Dear God, thank You for sending angels to protect me and keep me safe. Amen.

TODAY'S A GREAT DAY!

This is the day that the LORD has made. Let us rejoice and be glad today!

PSALM 118:24 NCV

When you think of celebrations, what do you think of? Birthdays and holidays? Maybe a big accomplishment, like winning a baseball game? Well, guess what? The Bible says every single day is a reason to celebrate, simply because God made it! Every day, God makes the sun rise and the birds sing. He makes the rain fall so plants can grow. He turns caterpillars into butterflies and decorates the night sky with stars. Even when things don't go your way, God is with you, all day every day. So celebrate! Because God made this a great day.

THOUGHT OF THE DAY

Can you name three things that make today great? Praise God for them!

PRAY TODAY

Dear God, thank You for today! You have made a beautiful world for me. Amen.

WHEN YOU LOOK IN THE MIRROR

As God has said: "I will live with them and walk among them, and I will be their God, and they will be my people."

2 CORINTHIANS 6:16 NIV

How do you feel when you look in the mirror? Do you like the person you see? God sure does! He loves you, inside and out.

When you accept God's love, He sends the Holy Spirit to live in your heart every single day. You are so special that God wants to hang out with you all the time!

If you're tempted to compare yourself with someone else, stop! God made you just as you should be. So try to see yourself the way God sees you: lovable and wonderful, just as you are.

THOUGHT OF THE DAY

Next time you look in the mirror, smile! You're an amazing creation!

PRAY TODAY

Dear God, thank You for making me unique and loving me so much. Help me love myself too! Amen.

SPEAK FROM YOUR HEART

"The mouth speaks the things that are in the heart."

MATTHEW 12:34B ICB

Have you ever said something you wish you could take back? Unkind words make others sad. And they don't make you feel great, either! But God has some advice to help you. Fill your heart with good things!

The Bible says that whatever is in your heart will come out in the things you say. So if you spend all your time feeling angry or selfish, your words will probably be hurtful. But if you look for ways to be thankful, helpful, and kind, your words will show all those things too! So today, try turning your thoughts from mad to glad. Everyone will hear the difference!

THOUGHT OF THE DAY

It's so much easier to be kind when only good things fill your mind!

PRAY TODAY

Dear God, please help me fill my heart with good things. I want my words to make people happy! Amen.

ONE BIG HAPPY FAMILY

His unchanging plan has always been to adopt us into his own family by sending Jesus Christ to die for us. And he did this because he wanted to!

EPHESIANS 1:5 TLB

God loves families! Every family looks a little bit different because every person is a little bit different. But from the very beginning, God's plan was for us to live in loving families where everyone takes care of each other.

And God's greatest plan of all is to make each of us part of His family! He watches over us and cares for us like a wonderful mom or dad does. And He wants us to support each other like brothers and sisters too! Take a look around. Is there someone you can share God's family-love with today?

THOUGHT OF THE DAY

Families can be big or small, but God's family has room for all!

PRAY TODAY

Dear God, thank You for inviting everyone to be part of Your family! I love You. Amen.

BETTER TOGETHER

Two can accomplish more than twice as much as one, for the results can be much better. If one falls, the other pulls him up; but if a man falls when he is alone, he's in trouble.

ECCLESIASTES 4:9–10 TLB

What do you like to do with your friends? Play pretend? Build things? Make up new games? Friends make everything better! And not because they always do what we say or let us have our own way. Friends have the most fun when we listen to each other's ideas and create something together!

God says that when people are true friends, they can do amazing things. By working together, we can build and solve and imagine things that no one could do all alone. And if we make mistakes, our friends help us make things right again. True friends are gifts from God!

THOUGHT OF THE DAY

Who is one of your true friends? Thank God for him or her today!

PRAY TODAY

Dear God, thank You for friendship! Please help me to be a true friend today and every day. Amen.

FEAR NOT!

So we will not be afraid even if the earth shakes, or the mountains fall into the sea.

PSALM 46:2 NCV

Do you ever feel afraid? Sometimes scary things happen, but God doesn't want you to be afraid. He wants you to know that no matter what happens, He will take care of you. In fact, God thought it was so important that the words "fear not" appear 365 times in the Bible. That's once for each day of the year!

Fear will try to trick you and make you believe that bad things will happen to you, but God says don't listen to fear. Instead, choose to be brave and trust Him. God will always take care of you!

THOUGHT OF THE DAY

Fear is a bully that you can defeat with faith!

PRAY TODAY

Dear God, whenever I feel afraid, I will remember that You said to "fear not." Thank You for helping me defeat fear with faith. Amen.

LISTEN TO WISDOM

My child, listen to what I say and remember what I command you. Listen carefully to wisdom; set your mind on understanding.

PROVERBS 2:1–2 NCV

Do you have lots to say? That's great! But don't forget to listen too!

God wants us to learn new things, so He asks us to listen to wisdom. You can do that by sitting quietly when your parents or teachers are speaking. Open your ears to hear all they say. Be sure you're not just waiting for your next chance to talk. And if you have questions, ask! When you let others speak and take time to hear their words, you can learn all kinds of things.

THOUGHT OF THE DAY

Wisdom is everywhere! Instead of hopping up right after dinner, stick around and listen to the conversation!

PRAY TODAY

Dear God, sometimes it's hard to listen when I want to talk! Please give me patience and help me hear wisdom. Amen.

DON'T WORRY, KEEP PRAYING

Do not worry about anything, but pray and ask God for everything you need, always giving thanks.

PHILIPPIANS 4:6 NCV

Everyone feels worried sometimes. God wants to help! So He gives us good advice in the Bible: pray.

He even tells us how to pray! First, tell God what's worrying you and ask Him for courage and peace. Then, remember to give thanks.

Sometimes worry seems to hide the good things God's done. So look around and tell God "thank You!" for every good thing you notice. It could be as big as your mom's love or as small as a puppy snuggle. When you spend time thinking about God's good gifts, your worry will fade away!

THOUGHT OF THE DAY

How does it feel when you get worried? What's something you can always remember to be thankful for?

PRAY TODAY

Dear God, thank You for listening to me when I get worried. Help me see all the good things You've given me! Amen.

WISHING OR HOPING?

May the God of hope fill you with all joy and peace as you trust in him, so that you may overflow with hope by the power of the Holy Spirit.

ROMANS 15:13 NIV

Have you ever wished for something? Sometimes people make wishes on a birthday candle or on a star. They think that if they wish really, really hard they will get what they want. But after they finish wishing, they start worrying that their wishes won't come true!

Hoping is different from wishing. The Bible tells us that hope is putting our trust in God, who loves us and always wants the best for us. When we trust in God to give us His very best, we can stop worrying. Hope fills us with joy and peace instead!

THOUGHT OF THE DAY

Trusting in God will help you rest, because He gives you what is best!

PRAY TODAY

Dear God, I am so thankful I don't need to worry, because my hope is in You. Amen.

STICKY SPIDER WEBS

"This is what you must do: Tell the truth to each other."

ZECHARIAH 8:16A NLT

A wise man once said that when we tell lies, it is like getting stuck in a sticky spider web. One lie leads to more lies, and soon we're all tangled up and trapped like a fly in a spider's web. But the Bible gives us good advice. God says to tell the truth to each other. When we choose to tell the truth, we never have to be worried about being trapped in a sticky web of lies. Telling the truth keeps us free. It is always the best thing to do.

THOUGHT OF THE DAY

Lies will always trap us, but the truth will make us free!

PRAY TODAY

Dear God, please help me make the right choice and always tell the truth. Amen.

A PROMISE YOU CAN SEE

"The rainbow that I have put in the sky will be my sign to you and to every living creature on earth."

GENESIS 9:12 CEV

God makes some important promises in the Bible. But one promise came with a picture: a rainbow!

God told Noah to build a giant boat (an "ark") and fill it with animals. Then God sent a huge flood to cover the whole world. But because Noah and his family obeyed God, they stayed safe. Afterward, God painted a rainbow in the sky as a promise. He promised never to flood the world again—and He never has!

You can't see every promise God makes. But every time you see a rainbow, you can remember that God's promises are real, and they're all around you!

THOUGHT OF THE DAY

Larry's favorite promise is that God will always be around! What's your favorite promise?

PRAY TODAY

Dear God, thank You for Your wonderful promises to me! Amen.

YOUR SPECIAL GIFT

This is why I remind you to keep using the gift God gave you . . .

2 TIMOTHY 1:6A NCV

Isn't it fun to open a gift? And it's even more fun to use it! Did you know that God gives each of us gifts? But they're not in boxes or bags. God's gifts are special abilities we can use to become the person He's created us to be.

Maybe you love to draw, or are good at music, reading, or math. Perhaps you're great at helping people or listening. There are all kinds of gifts God gives His children. Ask for His help to discover them and use them as you grow!

THOUGHT OF THE DAY

What do you think your gift from God might be? How can you use it as you grow?

PRAY TODAY

Dear God, thank You for giving me special gifts. Help me to work at using my gift for You and others. Amen.

TWO EARS AND ONE MOUTH

My dear brothers and sisters, always be willing to listen and slow to speak.

JAMES 1:19 NCV

Someone once said that we have two ears and one mouth, because we should listen twice as much as we talk! That's a funny way to say it, but did you know that the Bible also says we should listen more than we talk? Why do you think that is?

Listening is how we learn and understand. And it's also a way to show we care about someone. If we speak without listening, we might hurt someone's feelings! Listening first is God's way to show respect and love for others. Give it a try!

THOUGHT OF THE DAY

Listen to hear what others say. Then when you speak, others will listen to you!

PRAY TODAY

Dear God, sometimes it is hard for me to listen. Please help me give others time to speak before I do. Amen.

GOD'S GOOD PLANS

"I know what I am planning for you," says the LORD. "I have good plans for you, not plans to hurt you. I will give you hope and a good future."

JEREMIAH 29:11 NCV

Do you like thinking about what you will be when you grow up? Maybe you even enjoy pretending to be a firefighter, a ballerina, a teacher, an astronaut, or something else. It's wonderful to dream about—and even plan for!—what you will be one day.

You may not know just what you will become, but you can be sure that God has great plans for you. He loves you and wants only what is best for you. Pray every day and ask God to show you what He wants you to be. You can always trust God's plans.

THOUGHT OF THE DAY

What do you think you will do? Trust in God's good plans for you!

PRAY TODAY

Dear God, I am so glad that You have good plans for me. Please help me to follow Your ways each day. Amen.

FOR YOUR OWN GOOD

Losing self-control leaves you as helpless as a city without a wall.

PROVERBS 25:28 CEV

It's not always easy to follow the rules. Or to choose kind words. Or to be patient when you really, really want something! These are all times you need self-control. It takes practice, but God can help you!

Ask God to help you see the best choice in every situation. Some choices keep you safe—like looking both ways before you cross the street. Some keep others safe, like waiting patiently in line at the playground. Some choices are harder to see but just as important, like not spreading gossip and taking time to help others. Self-control keeps you healthy and happy! So keep practicing!

THOUGHT OF THE DAY

Can you think of a time self-control would keep you safe?

PRAY TODAY

Dear God, I want to get better at self-control. Will You please help me take the time to make good choices? Amen.

@ @ @ @ @ @ @

BE A FRIEND!

"Greater love has no one than this, that someone lay down his life for his friends."

JOHN 15:13 ESV

How can you keep good friends for a long time? The same way you make friends to begin with! Be a friend first.

The very best friends make sure to take care of each other. They listen carefully and pay attention to how the other person feels. They take turns choosing games and going first. And they work together when something is hard! Most important, good friends don't expect anything in return for doing nice things. They just enjoy doing nice things! So treat your friends the way you want to be treated. You'll always have a friend if you are one!

THOUGHT OF THE DAY

What can you do for a friend this week?

PRAY TODAY

Dear God, help me to be a great friend today and every day! Amen.

PRAY ABOUT EVERYTHING

Do not worry about anything, but pray and ask God for everything you need, always giving thanks.

PHILIPPIANS 4:6 NCV

Have you ever gotten a letter or a card in the mail? It's exciting! That's how God feels every time you pray. He loves to hear from you!

You don't have to wait until you need help with something to pray. Pray all the time! Tell God about your day, your family, and your friends. Tell Him what you're thinking about or tell Him something that happened today. God wants to spend time with you, and the more you talk to Him, the more you'll find things to say. After all, He is your best friend!

THOUGHT OF THE DAY

Tell God all about your day. He can't wait to hear from you!

PRAY TODAY

Dear God, I know You want to hear from me. Help me remember to pray all through my day. Amen.

@ ⊚ @ ⊚ @ @ ⊚

HOW TO BE STRONG

Finally, be strong in the Lord and in his mighty power.

EPHESIANS 6:10 NIV

People do all kinds of things to be strong. They exercise to build their muscles. They eat healthy food and get plenty of sleep. All of this helps make their bodies strong, but did you know there is another kind of strength? Being strong in the Lord is even more important than having strong muscles.

We get strong in the Lord by reading our Bibles, praying, and doing what God says. If you ask Him, God will teach you to follow Him and trust Him, and you will grow stronger each day. Nothing is greater than God's power. With Him, nothing is impossible!

THOUGHT OF THE DAY

Build your faith muscles by reading your Bible every day!

PRAY TODAY

Dear God, please help me learn to trust You more so I can be strong in You. Amen.

GOD CAN DO IT ALL

"God can do anything!"

LUKE 1:37 NCV

The Bible is full of stories about God's great miracles. He separated a huge sea so people could walk across on dry land. He made the sun move backwards. Jesus walked on water and stopped a scary storm!

But God's miracles aren't always big and showy. God also provided food for a poor, hungry woman and her son, and Jesus healed sick, lonely people and helped others change from being selfish to being generous. Nothing is too big or small for God. If you are having a hard time with something, ask God for help. He can do it all!

THOUGHT OF THE DAY

You can't do everything—but God can!

PRAY TODAY

Dear God, I'm so glad You can do anything! Thank You for all Your miracles, big and small. Amen.

PRAISING GOD

It is good to praise the LORD and make music to your name, O Most High.

PSALM 92:1 NIV

What is your favorite song? What kind of music do you like? One way to let God know how much we love Him is to make music and sing songs to Him. When you are happy, you can sing a happy song to God! But if you are sad, you can sing a sad song too, and God will love hearing it just as much. Any time we make music to God, we are praising Him. And the Bible says it is good to praise the Lord!

THOUGHT OF THE DAY

What song will you sing to God today?

PRAY TODAY

Dear God, I thank You for music and for giving me songs to sing. Please help me to praise You every day. Amen.

WALK IN TRUTH

I have no greater joy than this: to hear that my children are walking in the truth.

3 JOHN 1:4 HCSB

You probably know what it means to tell the truth. But what does God mean when He says we should *walk* in the truth?

He means that we should choose His ways all the time. So as you walk around today, look for ways you can follow God's direction. Treat people with His love and kindness. Help those who need it. Notice good things around you and thank God for them. Share God's love with your friends! When you walk through your day with God, you'll be sure to walk in the truth.

THOUGHT OF THE DAY

Walk with God and choose His way; He will guide you every day!

PRAY TODAY

Dear God, help me remember to walk with You all day so I can always walk in the truth. Amen.

A GIFT FOR GOD

The LORD is my strength and song; He has become my salvation. This is my God, and I will praise Him.

EXODUS 15:2 HCSB

It's fun to give gifts to people on holidays or birthdays, or even just because! But do you know you can also give God a special gift? You can give Him your praise!

Praising God means telling Him what you love about Him. You can do that by saying a prayer of thanks or singing a song about Him! You can draw a picture of something wonderful He's done for you. You can even dance for God! And you don't have to wait for a special day. Praise God every day! He's always happy to hear from you.

THOUGHT OF THE DAY

What can you praise God for today? Try singing a song about it!

PRAY TODAY

Dear God, I'm glad You love me so much! I praise You for all the ways You show Your love. Amen.

HOORAY FOR FRIENDS!

Every time I think of you, I give thanks to my God.

PHILIPPIANS 1:3 NLT

Friends are some of God's greatest gifts. A good friend can cheer you up when you feel sad, or help you finish a hard job. Friends can show you how to do something new. They can tell you funny stories and laugh at your jokes! And you can never have too many friends. There's always room for more!

It feels great to have good friends. So take time to thank God today for the ones He's given to you. And don't forget to be a good friend too!

THOUGHT OF THE DAY

Who is one of your good friends? How can you show you're thankful for their friendship?

PRAY TODAY

Dear God, thank You for my friends. Help me to be a good friend to each one! Amen.

PRAISE GOD ALWAYS!

My mouth is filled with your praise, and with your glory all the day.

PSALM 71:8 ESV

When you really love something, it's hard to stop talking about it. That's how we should feel about God!

Think about all the wonderful promises God has made. He will never leave you. He has big plans for you. He made you with special care, and gave you amazing gifts and talents. What an awesome God! So let's praise Him! Sing songs about His love, and share His greatness with your friends. Say prayers of thanks. You can even make up dances for Him! When you praise God, you remind your heart how great He is. So praise Him all day, every day!

THOUGHT OF THE DAY

Praise makes God happy—and it will make you happy too!

PRAY TODAY

Dear God, I love You! You give me all I need and You care for me so much. Thank You! Amen.

STRONG BODIES

You were bought by God for a price. So honor God with your bodies.

1 CORINTHIANS 6:20 NCV

God wants you to take good care of your body so that you can do all the wonderful things He has planned for you! Two important things you can do to be healthy and strong are eating good food and getting enough sleep. But something else you can do is move your body! Running, jumping, playing games, swimming, and dancing are some great ways to keep your body moving and healthy. Try different kinds of things until you find something you really enjoy. Then you will have fun while you build a strong body!

THOUGHT OF THE DAY

What kinds of activities do you enjoy to help your body be strong? What's something new you could try?

PRAY TODAY

Dear God, I want to take good care of my body so I can honor You. Help me make healthy choices today. Amen.

HOW TO BE HAPPY

I will be happy because of you; God Most High, I will sing praises to your name.

PSALM 9:2 NCV

Did you know there's a secret to happiness? Thankfulness! It's true. Happiness comes from loving God and thanking Him for what He's done.

Try it! Think about all the good things God has given you. Do you love your family? Did you have fun with a friend today? Do you live in a comfy home? When you take time to thank God, it's hard to feel upset. That's because your mind is too full of God's goodness to let anything else in! So next time you feel grouchy, remember: happiness is just a few thank-yous away!

THOUGHT OF THE DAY
What are three things you're thankful for today?

PRAY TODAY
Dear God, thank You for everything You've done for me! I love thinking about You and praising You. Amen.

THE BEST TEACHER

"Teacher, I will follow you wherever you go."

MATTHEW 8:19 ESV

D o you have a favorite teacher at school or church? What makes them a good teacher? Great teachers patiently help solve problems and explain things in fun or creative ways! And the best teachers also live as good examples.

The Bible tells us that Jesus was the very best teacher ever. He not only taught people how to live, but He loved them. He listened carefully to their problems. He treated each person with respect. And Jesus always lived so people could follow His perfect example. When you learn to do what Jesus teaches, you are following the very best teacher!

THOUGHT OF THE DAY

What are some lessons you have learned from the way Jesus lived?

PRAY TODAY

Dear Jesus, thank You for being my best teacher. I am so glad that You love me and help me with every problem. Amen.

HOW TO GET FAITH

So faith comes from hearing, and hearing through the word of Christ.

ROMANS 10:17 ESV

If you want to buy something, you can order it online or buy it in a store. But how do you get faith?

The Bible says that if we want to have faith, we need to listen to what God tells us—in the Bible! When we hear stories about Bible heroes and about Jesus' life, we learn how God loves and helps His people. We also learn about the promises God makes to help us and love us. We can trust the words in the Bible because they are true. And when we know the truth about God, our faith grows and grows!

THOUGHT OF THE DAY

God's Word makes faith grow.

PRAY TODAY

Dear God, thank You for giving us the Bible. Help my faith to grow as I listen to Your words and get to know You better. Amen.

CHOOSE YOUR THOUGHTS

"Those who are pure in their thinking are happy. They will be with God."

MATTHEW 5:8 ICB

You can't always choose what happens during your day. But you can choose how you think about it!

Try to find something good about whatever's going on. Is it raining when you were hoping to play outside? What a great day to splash in puddles! Did you have to miss your baseball game? Now you have more time to practice for next time! And if someone shares unkind gossip with you, don't spread it around. Keep your thoughts kind! God wants to give you peace and joy. Making sure your thoughts are happy can help you find God's great gifts!

THOUGHT OF THE DAY

Your thoughts tell your body how to feel.

PRAY TODAY

Dear God, please help me find good things to think about, no matter what's happening! Amen.

ALL KINDS OF FRIENDS

I will praise You because I have been remarkably and wonderfully made. Your works are wonderful, and I know this very well.

PSALM 139:14 HCSB

Everything God does is good. And He made everyone! So everyone you meet is one of God's good creations. Some people look different from others. Some people can't see, hear, or speak as easily as most. Some need to use extra help to get around—like a wheelchair. But none of that should stop you from being friends with all sorts of people! Ask kind questions. Invite them to play with you and your friends. Everyone deserves kindness and love. And you never know who could become your new best friend!

THOUGHT OF THE DAY

Wouldn't the world be boring if everyone was exactly the same?

PRAY TODAY

Dear God, please bring all kinds of people into my life. Thank You for making each of us so wonderfully! Amen.

NEW THINGS

"For I am about to do something new. See, I have already begun! Do you not see it?"

ISAIAH 43:19 NLT

Sometimes it is fun to do new things like start a new grade in school, get a new pet, learn something new, or go to a new place. But doing new things can sometimes be scary too. Who will be there? Will you make a friend? How will you know what to do? God promises to be with us when we start new things. He loves to help us when we are not sure what to do or what will happen next. So when you have something new to do, remember that God is right there, helping you shine!

THOUGHT OF THE DAY

What's something new you're trying?

PRAY TODAY

Dear God, I'm glad that You are always with me, especially when I do new things. Amen.

@ @ @ @ @ @ @

LET YOUR PATIENCE SHOW

Let your patience show itself perfectly in what you do. Then you will be perfect and complete and will have everything you need.

JAMES 1:4 NCV

Patience means waiting without getting angry. Sometimes that means waiting for something you want, like a birthday party or someone to play a game with you. And sometimes it means taking the time to do something well.

When you are learning something new, be patient with yourself! Try not to get discouraged if your drawings don't look like you'd hoped, or if it's hard to read new words, or if you can't play a sport as well as someone else. Keep trying! Let your patience show, and you'll get a little better each day.

THOUGHT OF THE DAY

Sometimes it helps to take a quick break, and then try again later!

PRAY TODAY

Dear God, sometimes I get so frustrated. Please help me be patient with myself so I can get better at new things. Amen.

FORGIVE THEM ANYWAY!

"When you are praying, and you remember that you are angry with another person about something, then forgive him. If you do this, then your Father in heaven will also forgive your sins."

MARK 11:25 ICB

When you forgive someone, it's really good for YOU! It sounds backwards, but it's true.

Anger grows and grows until you feel upset about everything! But choosing to forgive means you let go of your anger. You'll feel happier and more relaxed. Finally, you can stop thinking about that problem!

God asks us to forgive others when they do something wrong—even if they don't ask for it. So when you pray, start by asking God to help you forgive anyone who needs it. You'll be more peaceful and ready to hear what God has to say to you!

THOUGHT OF THE DAY

Forgiveness is one thing you never need permission for!

PRAY TODAY

Dear God, help me forgive others. I want to feel peaceful and hear Your voice! Amen.

JOY FROM GOD

But let all those rejoice who put their trust in You; Let them ever shout for joy, because You defend them; Let those also who love Your name Be joyful in You.

PSALM 5:11 NKJV

You might think being a king would be super fun. But King David's life wasn't always easy. In the book of Psalms, he wrote about feeling sad, confused, and even angry. But since he never stopped trusting God, he was still able to rejoice!

You can be joyful like King David too. That doesn't mean you need to be happy all the time. Sometimes it's hard to feel happy, isn't it? Joy comes from God and it's bigger than happiness. It means you trust that God will work things out, and you're excited for His plans. God can give you joy today. Just ask!

THOUGHT OF THE DAY

Give God your trust, and He'll give you His joy!

PRAY TODAY

Dear God, I want to have Your joy in my heart! Help me trust You more and more each day. Amen.

TRUTH TOOLS

Stand firm then, with the belt of truth buckled around your waist.

EPHESIANS 6:14A NIV

Do you ever feel like disobeying God? Or maybe He sometimes seems far away? The Bible says God gives us something special to help us stay strong: the Belt of Truth!

Think of the Belt of Truth like a cool tool belt that you can pack full of truths about God. Truth Tool #1: God loves you! Truth Tool #2: God wants you to treat others kindly. Fill your tool belt by learning Bible verses, listening to Bible stories, and talking with God. Then no matter what happens, you'll always be ready to whip out a Truth Tool!

THOUGHT OF THE DAY

What Truth Tool can you find in your favorite Bible story?

PRAY TODAY

Dear God, please help me learn Your truths so I can do the right thing and follow You no matter what! Amen.

TRY AGAIN

The LORD says, "Forget what happened before, and do not think about the past. Look at the new thing I am going to do. It is already happening. Don't you see it?"

ISAIAH 43:18–19A NCV

When was the last time you tried something new? Did you do it perfectly the first time? Of course not! Doing something well takes practice! When you try new things, you'll probably make a lot of mistakes. You might feel discouraged. You might even want to stop. But God says you should keep going!

What can you do differently next time? What can you learn from last time? God is with you, and He will use your mistakes to help you get better. But only if you keep working. So get back out there and try again!

THOUGHT OF THE DAY

With God's help, every mistake can become a wonderful lesson!

PRAY TODAY

Dear God, sometimes I get frustrated when I can't do something right. Please help me try again instead of giving up! Amen.

🌀 🌀 🌀 🌀 🌀 🌀 🌀 🌀

GOD CAN DO IT

Jesus looked at them intently, then said, "Without God, it is utterly impossible. But with God everything is possible."

MARK 10:27 TLB

The Bible tells us that when God's people were wandering in a desert without food and water, they called out to God. He made a special kind of food called manna fall from the sky. He even made water flow out of a rock. God can do what we think is impossible!

God wants to help you too. When you have a problem that is really hard or when you are afraid, things may seem impossible. But God can help. He loves you and wants to do wonderful things for you. Talk to God, then watch to see what He can do!

THOUGHT OF THE DAY

What is your favorite Bible story about God doing impossible things?

PRAY TODAY

Dear God, I am so glad that nothing is impossible for You! Thank You for loving me and helping me. Amen.

KINDNESS HELPS EVERYONE!

A kind person is doing himself a favor.

PROVERBS 11:17A ICB

When you think about kindness, you probably think about doing something nice for someone else. But kindness is good for you too! Especially when it means making a new friend.

When you invite someone to play with you, you are showing kindness to him or her. It feels so good to be included! And the bonus is, you're also showing kindness to yourself. Everyone has great ideas. Maybe this new friend can help you make up a brand-new game. Maybe you can help each other build a super-tall sand castle, or climb a tricky tree! Showing kindness is the perfect way to start a friendship.

THOUGHT OF THE DAY

Next time you're playing, look around. Is there someone who might like to be included?

PRAY TODAY

Dear God, I want to be kind. Please help me notice who is left out, and invite them to be my new friends! Amen.

A CHEERFUL HEART

A cheerful heart does good like medicine.

PROVERBS 17:22 TLB

When your tummy hurts or your nose is stuffy, medicine can help your body feel better. And when you're feeling sad or grouchy, thinking of something cheerful can make your heart feel better!

What makes you happy? Can you think of a song you love to sing? Can you remember a funny joke that makes you laugh? Sometimes just thinking about someone you love can cheer you up. So next time you feel yourself getting grumpy, try to fill your mind with things you like. It's like happiness medicine—you'll feel better in no time!

THOUGHT OF THE DAY

What's something that made you laugh today?

PRAY TODAY

Dear God, please help me find things to be cheerful about every day! Amen.

GOD KNOWS BEST

"Be strong and courageous. Do not be afraid or terrified because of them, for the LORD your God goes with you; he will never leave you nor forsake you."

DEUTERONOMY 31:6 NIV

Gideon was a soldier who wanted to please God. But one day, God told him to lead a tiny army against an enemy that had a huge army! Gideon felt scared, but God promised to help him. So Gideon did exactly what God said, and his army won the battle!

God might not ask you to lead an army. But maybe you need to do something else that takes courage—like moving to a new school or saying no when a friend wants you to break the rules. Ask God to help you feel brave. With Him, you can do anything!

THOUGHT OF THE DAY

Be brave and follow God. He's got the best ideas!

PRAY TODAY

Dear God, I want to be brave like Gideon. Please give me courage to do whatever You have in mind for me! Amen.

GROWING IN GOD

. . . so that you will live the kind of life that honors and pleases the Lord in every way. You will produce fruit in every good work and grow in the knowledge of God.

COLOSSIANS 1:10 NCV

Life with God is an amazing adventure. There's always something new to discover!

Even your Sunday school teachers and your pastors are still learning about God. That's because He does new things every day. Sometimes you'll think you totally understand something in the Bible, and then He'll show you a brand-new way to think about it! So never stop following God, asking questions, and learning about His wonderful ways. You never know what you might find!

THOUGHT OF THE DAY

God can help you learn and grow.
There's always something new to know!

PRAY TODAY

Dear God, I love being on this adventure with You! Help my knowledge of You grow a little more each day. Amen.

HAPPY INSIDE OUT

I'm happy from the inside out, and from the outside in, I'm firmly formed.

PSALM 16:9 MSG

How do you tell if someone is happy? Since we can't see feelings, we usually look at the outside to see how someone feels on the inside. If someone is stomping around with a frown on her face, we can be pretty sure that she's mad or sad. But when a person is feeling happy, he'll usually smile or laugh or sing or dance or even try to make others happy. The Bible says it's good to show your happy feelings from the inside out! So share your happiness with someone else today!

THOUGHT OF THE DAY

Turn your frown upside down, and share a smile today!

PRAY TODAY

Dear God, thank You for giving me so much to be happy about. Please help me to share my happiness from the inside out! Amen.

BRANCH OUT!

"Yes, I am the Vine; you are the branches. Whoever lives in me and I in him shall produce a large crop of fruit. For apart from me you can't do a thing."

JOHN 15:5 TLB

Have you ever seen a fruit tree? A strong trunk grows up from the ground, and many branches reach out from the top. The trunk delivers water to the branches so they can make tons of yummy fruit!

The Bible tells us that Jesus is like a strong trunk, and we should be like branches. When you stay connected to Him, He'll give you what you need to do great things! Find special times to spend with Jesus each day. Read a Bible story at breakfast. Sing a worship song at lunchtime. Pray before bed—or any time at all! Staying close to Jesus brings His wonderful blessings!

THOUGHT OF THE DAY

How can you spend special time with Jesus today?

PRAY TODAY

Dear Jesus, You have everything I need! Please help me stay close to You. Amen.

A GOOD EXAMPLE

"I have given you an example to follow. Do as I have done to you."

JOHN 13:15 NLT

D o you ever wonder how you should act? Just look at Jesus! In the Bible, Jesus says we can follow His example and treat people like He does. When you do that, *you* become an example too. Isn't that exciting?

But remember that none of us is perfect. So don't worry when you make mistakes! You can still be an example when you say sorry, fix what's wrong, and ask for forgiveness. Jesus wants us to follow His ways, share His love, and help where we can. When you are kind to everyone—including yourself!—you are doing exactly what He asked!

THOUGHT OF THE DAY

What's your favorite story about Jesus?

PRAY TODAY

Dear God, thank You for sending Jesus to be a perfect example for me to follow! Amen.

@ @ @ @ @ @ @ @

KEEP ON ASKING

When doubts filled my mind, your comfort gave me renewed hope and cheer.

PSALM 94:19 NLT

You probably have lots of questions about God. That's no problem! He has all the answers you need. Asking questions about God is called *seeking*. God wants us to seek Him, so don't ever be afraid to ask about things you don't understand. Talk to your parents or your Sunday school teacher. Be sure to read the Bible and ask God to make things clearer to you. The better you know God, the more comfort and joy you'll find in Him. So just keep on asking!

THOUGHT OF THE DAY

Jesus says that seeking leads to finding. So never stop seeking God!

PRAY TODAY

Dear God, please help me ask questions anytime I feel uncertain. Thank You for listening and answering! Amen.

SHARE GOD'S LOVE

"If you have two shirts, share with the person who does not have one. If you have food, share that too."

LUKE 3:11 ICB

What can you share with others? Clothes you don't wear much? Toys you don't play with? Sharing with others feels great. Even better, it's what God wants us to do!

God asks us to take care of each other by sharing what we have. You may not think you have much to give, but even small gifts can make a big difference. The Bible tells a story of a little boy who gave his small lunch to Jesus. Jesus used it to feed 5,000 people!

Ask God to show you how to share the things you have. He could help you change someone's life!

THOUGHT OF THE DAY

When you share with others, you share more than just things—you share God's love!

PRAY TODAY

Dear God, thank You for everything You've given me. Please help me share what I have with others. Amen.

RIGHT ON TIME

He has made everything beautiful in its time.

ECCLESIASTES 3:11 NIV

Sometimes it feels like God moves really slowly. Sometimes it might even seem like He's not doing anything! But don't worry. God is always at work, helping you grow and learn. He has wonderful plans for you!

Talk to God about the things you want. Tell Him how hard it is to wait and ask for His help! Then watch for Him during your day. Did a friend say something encouraging? Are you getting closer to mastering a new skill? Was today happier than yesterday? God won't let you down. When you trust Him, He'll show up right on time!

THOUGHT OF THE DAY

God will give you exactly what you need at exactly the right time.

PRAY TODAY

Dear God, sometimes it's hard to see You working. Help me trust that Your timing is the best timing. Amen.

EVERYONE DESERVES RESPECT

Show respect for all people.

1 PETER 2:17A ICB

You've probably heard that you should respect your parents and teachers. But did you know that everyone deserves respect? That's because God made each person with great love.

Respect means that you care how another person feels. That doesn't mean you have to be best friends with everyone. But you can speak with kindness. You can choose words and actions that build others up, and you can always apologize when you make a mistake. Respect is one of the best ways to obey God and show His love.

THOUGHT OF THE DAY

Everyone includes YOU! Don't forget to show yourself respect and kindness every day.

PRAY TODAY

Dear God, I'm glad You love everyone. Help me remember to respect all people—not just the ones I like most! Amen.

GOD'S PROMISE

"I assure you: Anyone who believes has eternal life."

JOHN 6:47 HCSB

God has made a great big promise: He will never leave you. In fact, He sent us His Son, Jesus, so that no one would ever have to be apart from Him. When you believe in Jesus, God lives in your heart every single day. And you get to live in heaven with Him forever!

Nothing will ever come between you and God. You can't lose Him, and He doesn't take breaks. Wherever you go, He is with you. No matter how many mistakes you make, He won't give up on you. His love is forever. That's a promise!

THOUGHT OF THE DAY

The gift of God's promise is free for everyone! All you have to do is say yes.

PRAY TODAY

Dear God, thank You for sending Jesus so we can always be together. I'm glad Your love is forever! Amen.

HEAR YOUR FAITH

So faith comes from hearing, that is, hearing the Good News about Christ.

ROMANS 10:17 NLT

Faith means believing in something we can't see. It's not always easy. But the Bible gives us a simple way to have more faith: hear the Good News of Jesus!

When you hear about all the things Jesus said and did, you'll start to understand His love for you. You can hear about Jesus at church, of course. But you don't have to wait for Sunday! Ask your mom or dad to help you read Bible stories every day. Listen to worship songs, or make up your own! Every time you hear about Jesus your faith will grow a little more.

THOUGHT OF THE DAY

A devotional book like this one is a great way to hear the Good News too!

PRAY TODAY

Dear God, when I hear about Jesus, please help me really listen. I want my faith to grow!
Amen.

CAREFUL LISTENING

Listen carefully to wisdom; set your mind on understanding.

PROVERBS 2:2 NCV

Every day you hear many different things. Some things are true, and some are not. If you are a careful listener, you will be able to understand who is telling you the truth and who is not. God wants us to listen to people who can be trusted.

Some trustworthy people are your parents, or your grandparents. Others are good teachers who help you learn and good coaches who help you play better. Good friends help you grow and understand new things too. When you listen to wise, kind people, you will discover true things that will help you become who God wants you to be.

THOUGHT OF THE DAY

Who is someone you know who can be trusted to tell the truth?

PRAY TODAY

Dear God, help me remember to be a careful listener and to grow to understand the truth. Amen.

IT'S ALL FORGOTTEN

You will throw away all our sins into the deepest part of the sea.

MICAH 7:19B NCV

If you want to know what true forgiveness looks like, just watch how God does it. He doesn't secretly stay mad while pretending everything is OK. He doesn't remind us of our mistakes all the time. Instead, when we tell God we're sorry, He just forgives us—right away and all the way! In fact, the Bible says it's like God throws our sins to the bottom of the ocean where no one can reach them. He doesn't pay attention to them anymore! We get a fresh new start with God anytime we ask. Isn't that wonderful news?

THOUGHT OF THE DAY

God's forgiveness is forever!

PRAY TODAY

Dear God, thank You for forgiving me no matter what! Help me to forgive others just like You: right away and all the way! Amen.

SNEAK ATTACK!

Two are better than one, because they get more done by working together.

ECCLESIASTES 4:9 NCV

God loves for you to obey your parents and help others when they ask you to. But He's *really* happy when you help *without* being asked! Can you do that?

Think of it like sneak-attack helping. Maybe your mom is extra busy with work one night. Sneak attack! You can set the table for dinner. Maybe your friend has to finish her chores before she can play. Sneak attack! Share the chores, and start playing sooner! Sneak-attack helpfulness makes everyone's day better.

THOUGHT OF THE DAY

Everyone needs a hand sometimes. Where will your next sneak attack be?

PRAY TODAY

Dear God, please show me ways I can be helpful every day—even before someone asks! Amen.

BE A LIGHT

"You are the light of the world. A town built on a hill cannot be hidden. . . . Let your light shine before others, that they may see your good deeds and glorify your Father in heaven."

MATTHEW 5:14-16 NIV

I f you are hiking in the dark, you cannot see where to go. But if you have a flashlight, you can turn it on. Then you can see the right way to go! In the Bible, Jesus calls His followers "the light of the world." What that means is that when we do what Jesus says, we become like a light, shining in the dark, so others can see the way to go.

When you live Jesus' way, you help others see God. You become a "light" where you live, play, and learn, by doing the right thing.

THOUGHT OF THE DAY

How could you be a "light" for someone you know?

PRAY TODAY

Dear God, please help me to shine brightly for You so others know You love them too. Amen.

DANIEL'S CHOICE

But Daniel made up his mind that he would not defile himself . . .

DANIEL 1:8 NASB

Daniel was a Bible hero who had to make some hard choices. He had to decide whether he would obey God's laws or obey the laws of a bad king named Darius. If Daniel chose to obey God, King Darius would get mad! It was a scary choice, but Daniel decided to obey God instead of the king.

Angry King Darius threw Daniel into a pit with hungry lions. But God shut the lions' mouths and protected Daniel! Then Darius knew that Daniel's God was more powerful than any king on earth! God took care of Daniel because Daniel chose to obey Him.

THOUGHT OF THE DAY

Choosing to obey God isn't always easy, but it is always the right thing to do.

PRAY TODAY

Dear God, help me make good choices each day. I want to follow Jesus and do what is right. Amen.

RIGHT BESIDE YOU

"Fear not, for I am with you; Be not dismayed, for I am your God. I will strengthen you."

ISAIAH 41:10A NKJV

When you're with your friends or family, how do you feel? It's easy to feel happy, confident, and even brave with people who love you. The good news is, you can feel that way all the time! That's because God is always with you.

There may be times you feel lonely, but God is right beside you. And He says you never have to feel afraid or worried, because He'll never leave! So ask for His help. Tell Him your thoughts and feelings. Then trust Him to make you strong!

THOUGHT OF THE DAY

God will never try to hide. He's forever by your side!

PRAY TODAY

Dear God, I love You! Thank You for being with me all day, every day. Amen.

SMILE POWER!

Smiling faces make you happy, and good news makes you feel better.

PROVERBS 15:30 GNT

Did you know that you have a special power that can help people feel better? The Bible says that smiling faces and good news make you feel better. When you share a smile, a joke, or a funny story, you show you have a cheerful heart. And that makes others feel better. Maybe you can even sing one of Larry's silly songs to make a friend laugh! Look around and see who might need cheering up. Then use your "smile power" to help them feel better.

THOUGHT OF THE DAY

How can you cheer up a friend or someone in your family today?

PRAY TODAY

Dear God, thanks for giving me a cheerful heart. Help me to share some smiles today so others will feel better. Amen.

CONFIDENT WITH GOD

For the LORD will be your confidence, and will keep your foot from being caught.

PROVERBS 3:26 NKJV

Have you ever gotten really good at something? It takes practice! But when you are sure you can do something well, that's called being confident. And it feels great.

God wants us to be confident in making good choices. You can do that by checking in with God during your day. How would He want you to treat a new friend? Are your words helpful or hurtful? What does God say about keeping promises and working hard? When you practice living God's way, He'll give you the confidence to do it every day!

THOUGHT OF THE DAY

You can be confident that God's way is always the best way!

PRAY TODAY

Dear God, please give me confidence to live each day the way You want me to. Amen.

THE BEST SURPRISE

"I say to you who are listening to me, love your enemies. Do good to those who hate you. Ask God to bless those who say bad things to you. Pray for those who are cruel to you."

LUKE 6:27–28 ICB

Jesus was always surprising people with His actions. But one of His biggest surprises was something He said: love your enemies.

You can't always control how people treat you. But you *can* choose how you respond. If people are mean to you, they might expect you to be mean in return. But you can surprise them, just like Jesus did! Choose kind words and actions instead. You can even pray for them and ask Jesus to help you forgive them! Kindness and forgiveness are the best surprises.

THOUGHT OF THE DAY

Whom can you surprise with kindness and forgiveness today?

PRAY TODAY

Dear God, sometimes it's hard to be kind when others aren't. Please help me remember to love and forgive. Amen.

NEVER ALONE

"Be sure of this—that I am with you always, even to the end of the world."

MATTHEW 28:20B TLB

Do you ever feel alone? Maybe your best friend can't come over to play and you feel lonely. You may have to stay with a babysitter when your parents go to work or away for a while. These are all great times to remember that God is always with you.

The Bible tells us that God never leaves us. He is with us every single day and night, no matter where we are. Isn't that wonderful to know? Next time you are feeling lonely, remember these words from God: "I am with you always!"

THOUGHT OF THE DAY

God promises He'll never leave you—and He always keeps His promises!

PRAY TODAY

Dear God, I am so glad that You never leave me. Help me remember to ask You for help when I feel alone or afraid. Amen.

HE IS EVERYWHERE

God did this so that [people] would seek him and perhaps reach out for him and find him, though he is not far from any one of us.

ACTS 17:27 NIV

You can talk to God anytime you want to. That's because He's everywhere!

God isn't like you and me. He doesn't need to take a bike or car or airplane to get places. God is always with you, wherever you are. And He loves to hear from you! So turn to God anytime you feel afraid or discouraged. He is there. Praise Him when you feel thankful. He is there. Your whole life, no matter where you go or what you do, God will be right beside you. All you have to do is talk to Him!

THOUGHT OF THE DAY

You are never far away from God.

PRAY TODAY

Dear God, I love knowing that You are everywhere I go. Thank You for listening to all my prayers! Amen.

LOVE FORGIVES

Love is kind and patient, never jealous, boastful, proud, or rude. Love isn't selfish or quick-tempered. It doesn't keep a record of wrongs that others do.

1 CORINTHIANS 13:4–5 CEV

Sometimes when others say mean things, we want to say mean things right back to them. If they push ahead of us in line, we might feel like pushing them too. These kinds of things might feel right to us, but the Bible says that if we want to show love, we should forgive.

Forgiving someone means that we don't say angry words back, we don't push back, and we don't always have to have our own way. We treat others with kindness, just like we want to be treated. It's not easy, but God can help you!

THOUGHT OF THE DAY

How can you show love when someone hasn't been loving to you?

PRAY TODAY

Dear God, I'm so glad You always love and forgive me. Please help me remember to love and forgive others. Amen.

DON'T JUST STAND THERE

But be doers of the word, and not hearers only.

JAMES 1:22 NKJV

God wants us to read the Bible and listen carefully to pastors and teachers. But listening isn't enough. Once you've heard what God says, then get up and do something about it!

In the story of Esther, God tells us to stand up for what's right. Can you speak kindly when others want to gossip? The story of the Good Samaritan shows us that helping people makes God happy. How can you help someone? When you do what God says, it shows that you've really heard Him. So don't just stand there! Do something for God!

THOUGHT OF THE DAY

What's your favorite Bible story? What could it be telling you to do?

PRAY TODAY

Dear God, I want to be a hearer AND a doer of Your Word. Thank You for giving me such great directions in the Bible! Amen.

CHOOSING TO FORGIVE

Be gentle and ready to forgive; never hold grudges. Remember, the Lord forgave you, so you must forgive others. Most of all, let love guide your life.

COLOSSIANS 3:13-14 TLB

What if someone hurts your feelings, but then later says they're sorry? You have a choice: you can choose to stay mad or choose to forgive and be friends again. What would you do?

God says it is good to forgive others and not stay mad. It's not always easy, but we can ask God for help. Remember that God always forgives us when we are sorry for doing something wrong. He's the expert! And since He wants us to follow His ways, He can help us do just that. It's loving and kind to forgive, and it makes God happy too!

THOUGHT OF THE DAY

Saying "sorry" and forgiving is the way to happy living!

PRAY TODAY

Dear God, thank You for always forgiving me. Please help me to choose to forgive others. Amen.

@ @ @ @ @ @ @ @

GIVE JOYFULLY

"Freely you have received; freely give."

MATTHEW 10:8B NIV

God loves to give us what we need. And He loves to see us care for people! In fact, He's happiest when we use His gifts to help others.

Do you have lots of toys? Ask your parents to help you choose a few nice things to give away to families who don't have as much. Do you love art? Create birthday cards (or crafts!) for everyone in your family. Are sports fun and easy for you? Help a friend or sibling learn to play! When you give joyfully, you share more than your stuff—you share God's love!

THOUGHT OF THE DAY

What's a wonderful gift someone has given to you?

PRAY TODAY

Dear God, please help me share what I have with anyone who needs it! Amen.

A PLACE FOR YOU

You are my hiding place and my shield; I hope in your word.

PSALM 119:114 NCV

D o you have a favorite place where you feel safe? Maybe it's a treehouse, a garden, or tucked in tight at bedtime. When you're feeling upset, sometimes a special place where you can be alone helps you feel better.

God says that He is our hiding place. That means that you can go to Him any time you need help. If you feel scared, He can comfort you. If you feel lonely, He will never leave your side. You may not be able to climb into bed every time you feel sad, but you can imagine climbing into God's arms. He is your special place, wherever you go.

THOUGHT OF THE DAY
When you feel scared, God is only a prayer away!

PRAY TODAY
Dear God, thank You for being a safe place for me, wherever I am. I love You. Amen.

GOD GIVES GOOD THINGS

For the LORD God is our sun and our shield. He gives us grace and glory. The LORD will withhold no good thing from those who do what is right.

God always gives His children good things. He provides sunshine and rain so things can grow. He gives us families so that we can be loved. He gives us homes to live in so we can feel safe. He gives us bodies that can do many amazing things. He helps us learn and grow, sleep and play. And best of all, He gives us His love so that we can know Him and live with Him forever. God wants to give us every good thing because He is a loving Father to all His children!

THOUGHT OF THE DAY

Name three good things God has given you!

PRAY TODAY

Dear God, thank You so much for being my loving heavenly Father and for giving me so many good things. Amen.

FORGIVING MAKES THINGS BETTER

Be kind and compassionate to one another, forgiving each other, just as in Christ God forgave you.

EPHESIANS 4:32 NIV

Sometimes when we've done something wrong, we feel bad about it. We might want to hide or pretend we didn't do it, but that doesn't make the feeling go away. God makes a way for us to feel better. It is called forgiveness!

It's simple. You can go to the person you have hurt, tell them what you have done, and ask them to forgive you. When we say "sorry" and ask for forgiveness, we always feel better. God says that giving and receiving forgiveness are wonderful ways to show kindness to one another.

THOUGHT OF THE DAY

God forgives, and so should we!

PRAY TODAY

Dear God, thank You for forgiving me. Please help me ask for forgiveness when I have done something wrong. Amen.

GENTLE WORDS

A gentle answer turns away anger, but a sharp word causes anger.

PROVERBS 15:1 NLV

The Bible says we should be gentle, even when we feel angry. The problem is, that's pretty hard to do when you feel really mad! So God gives us some help. He says we don't have to feel gentle all the time. All we need to do is choose gentle words.

Instead of shouting or hitting, try explaining why you're upset, or ask for some alone time. If you do say something unkind, say "I'm sorry" right away. You'll probably start to feel better, and so will the other person. Gentle words can calm everyone down—including yourself!

THOUGHT OF THE DAY

You can't choose how you feel. You can choose how you talk about it!

PRAY TODAY

Dear God, sometimes I get so mad I choose the wrong words. Please help me speak gently so together we can make things better! Amen.

WHO'S FIRST?

Don't be selfish. . . . Be humble, thinking of others as better than yourself.

PHILIPPIANS 2:3 TLB

Do you like being the line leader or being chosen first on a team? It feels special to be first, but the Bible shows us a way to be even more special. It's called being humble. When we are humble, we let others go first. That's what Jesus did!

Jesus was God's Son, and that made Him the most special person who ever lived. But He knew that putting others first showed them how special they were to God. What an amazing gift to give! It isn't always easy to let others go first, but it's a great way to be more like Jesus!

THOUGHT OF THE DAY

What are some ways you can show others they are special?

PRAY TODAY

Dear God, please help me to put others first even when it isn't easy. Help me be more like You. Amen.

BIG DREAMS

Now glory be to God, who by his mighty power at work within us is able to do far more than we would ever dare to ask or even dream of—infinitely beyond our highest prayers, desires, thoughts, or hopes.

EPHESIANS 3:20 TLB

Have you ever had big dreams about what you would like to be when you grow up? Maybe you dream about being a firefighter or a teacher or a dancer or an astronaut. The Bible says that God loves you, and He has big dreams for you too. He wants to help you have a wonderful life when you grow up! Because He made you, He knows what is best for you and how to help you. Stay close to God so that you and He will accomplish your big dreams together!

THOUGHT OF THE DAY

God has the power to make big dreams come true!

PRAY TODAY

Dear God, thank You for loving me and for giving me hope for a wonderful future with You! Amen.

@ @ @ @ @ @ @

DO IT NOW!

"All of us must quickly carry out the tasks assigned us by the one who sent me, for there is little time left before the night falls and all work comes to an end."

JOHN 9:4 TLB

What do you do when your mom asks you to pick up your toys? When you are playing outside and your dad calls you to come inside, do you come right away? When it's time for school, do you get your things together quickly so you're ready to go? When we each do our jobs quickly, the whole family is happier. Waiting or whining just makes things take longer. Next time someone asks you to help out, see how fast you can get it done. If you do it now, you won't have to worry about doing it later!

THOUGHT OF THE DAY
It's much more fun to get things done!

PRAY TODAY
Dear God, I want to be a good worker. Please help me to do things right away instead of waiting. Amen.

PICK JESUS

"Follow Me," Jesus told them, "and I will make you fish for people!" Immediately they left their nets and followed Him.

MARK 1:17–18 HCSB

Who are some good leaders in your life? Do you have a teacher who explains things well? Maybe your parents help you make smart choices when you're feeling confused. When you choose to follow a good leader, you'll never get lost!

Jesus is the best leader of all. When we follow Him, we learn to be kind and brave. He shows us the best ways to help others, and guides us through difficult times. And He will lead you to amazing blessings! Jesus knows the way to your very best life. So stay close to Him!

THOUGHT OF THE DAY
Jesus knows the way; just follow Him each day!

PRAY TODAY
Dear Jesus, please help me choose to follow You every day. You always lead me to good things! Amen.

FRIENDS WHO MAKE YOU BETTER

As iron sharpens iron, so people can improve each other.

PROVERBS 27:17 NCV

What are some things you like about your friends? The Bible says that great friends help each other be the very best they can be. They encourage each other to do good and work hard. God wants you to find those kinds of friends. They build you up and help you grow!

If a friend ever pushes you to do something wrong, he or she isn't a very good friend. Be firm, and say no. Then look for friends who are kind and will help you make good decisions. You'll be glad you did!

THOUGHT OF THE DAY

Who is one of your good friends? What do you like to do together?

PRAY TODAY

Dear God, please help me make friends who are kind and encouraging. And help me to be that kind of friend too! Amen.

THE GIFT OF FORGIVENESS

"I will forgive their wrongdoings, and I will never again remember their sins."

HEBREWS 8:12 CSB

One of God's best gifts is forgiveness! And we can have it any time we need it.

We all have rules we need to follow. And when you break the rules, it doesn't feel great, does it? If you keep it a secret, you might feel yucky inside. If you hurt someone else, it might make you feel sad. You might even get in trouble. But God will always forgive you. All you have to do is ask! Then, He can fill you with courage to make things right, and to do better next time. His love is bigger than any mistakes we make!

THOUGHT OF THE DAY

God forgives you right away. The gift is free, so ask today!

PRAY TODAY

Dear God, thank You for the awesome gift of forgiveness. Please help me talk to You right away when I make mistakes. Amen.

@ @ @ @ @ @ @

MAKING MISTAKES

"You're blessed when you're content with just who you are—no more, no less."

MATTHEW 5:5 MSG

God made you. He loves you, and He has great plans for you. He wants you to become the person He created you to be. But that doesn't mean you will never make mistakes. In fact, making mistakes is just another way to grow.

When you are learning to kick a ball or draw a picture, to ride a bike or read a book, you won't always get it right. That is perfectly OK! If you keep on trying, you will get better. Be happy that you are growing and learning. That's just how God planned it!

THOUGHT OF THE DAY

Can you name three things that you are learning to do?

PRAY TODAY

Dear God, I'm glad You made me and that You love me. Help me keep trying, even when I make mistakes. Amen.

PERFECT TIMING

But they that wait upon the Lord shall renew their strength; they shall mount up with wings as eagles; they shall run, and not be weary; and they shall walk, and not faint.

ISAIAH 40:31 KJV

God knows what you need and when you need it. He loves you! And He promises to help you learn and grow so you can do the great things He's planned for you.

Sometimes it can feel like God moves really slowly. Maybe you're impatient to know what God has in store for you. Or you have big dreams that you want to do RIGHT NOW! But the Bible says that when we wait for God to help us, we'll be able to do much more than we can even imagine. That's exciting! So trust God. His timing is perfect!

THOUGHT OF THE DAY

God's timing isn't the same as our timing—it's better!

PRAY TODAY

Dear God, thank You for making big plans for me! Help me to be patient and trust Your timing. Amen.

THE ONE AND ONLY YOU!

For you created my inmost being; you knit me together in my mother's womb. I praise you because I am fearfully and wonderfully made.

PSALM 139:13 NIV

God worked really hard to make you. He gave you a smile that only you have. He made your eyes and ears and nose unique. He chose your hair color and decided where to put each freckle—or maybe decided you wouldn't have freckles at all! God lovingly designed you to be exactly the way you are. There is only one you!

So don't believe anyone who says you should look or act or sound a certain way. The world needs you just how you are. That's why God made you that way!

THOUGHT OF THE DAY

What's something special about you?

PRAY TODAY

Dear God, thank You for all the ways You made me special. I love being Your child! Amen.

BEING FRIENDS

Be kind to each other, tenderhearted, forgiving one another, just as God through Christ has forgiven you.

EPHESIANS 4:32 NLT

The Bible tells us that friendship is very important. Jesus even calls His followers His friends! But if we want to have good friends, we have to be willing to be a good friend.

Friends are kind and take care of one another. Friends forgive when they make mistakes. Friends tell each other the truth. If you look for ways to treat others the way you would like to be treated, you will always have good friends. And you'll be a good friend too!

THOUGHT OF THE DAY

Can you name some of your good friends? What is it that makes them such good friends?

PRAY TODAY

Dear God, I am so glad You have given me good friends. Will You please help me to be a good friend too? Amen.

BEING THANKFUL

I said to myself, "Relax and rest. God has showered you with blessings."

PSALM 116:7 MSG

You probably know it's polite to say "thank you" when you get a birthday gift. But you get all sorts of gifts every single day! Your parents give you love, a home, good food, and many other things. Do you remember to say "thank you" to them?

And don't forget about God! When you look at the world around you, try to notice all the amazing things that God has given you. Birds, rainbows, puffy white clouds, shady trees, warm sunshine, and oceans are just a few of His blessings. So remember to thank God each day too!

THOUGHT OF THE DAY

Can you name five blessings God has given you?

PRAY TODAY

Dear God, You are so amazing. I just want to thank You for everything You have given to me! Amen.

🌀 🌀 🌀 🌀 🌀 🌀 🌀 🌀

KEEP ON TRYING

"Continue to ask, and God will give to you. Continue to search, and you will find. Continue to knock, and the door will open for you."

MATTHEW 7:7 ICB

When you play "Hide and Seek," do you give up if you don't find someone right away? At soccer practice, do you quit if you miss the ball? No way! When you want to get better at something, you need to keep on trying.

So if we want to know God better, we need to keep working on that too. We get to know God better when we read the Bible, learn about Jesus, and when we talk to Him in prayer. God promises to help us know Him better if we keep on trying.

THOUGHT OF THE DAY

God loves it when we look for Him. What are you doing to learn more about Him?

PRAY TODAY

Dear God, I want to know You better and better. Thank You for loving me. Amen.

FOLLOW THE CLUES

Now, Israel, listen to the laws and commands I will teach you. Obey them so that you will live.

DEUTERONOMY 4:1 NCV

Do you ever have a hard time following directions? Sometimes you may not even want to listen in the first place! But God gives us rules and directions that are meant to give us a wonderful life. So it's a good idea to listen as carefully as you can.

Think of the Bible as a treasure hunt. Each time God gives a direction, it's a clue to get you one step closer to all He's planned for you. Pretty soon, just by following His directions, you'll find amazing treasures: joy, peace, and a great friendship with God!

THOUGHT OF THE DAY

The Ten Commandments could also be called ten clues to a great life! Check them out today.

PRAY TODAY

Dear God, thank You for giving us the Bible, so I can follow Your good directions! Amen.

SHARING BLESSINGS

Every good gift and every perfect gift is from above, and comes down from the Father of lights.

JAMES 1:17 NKJV

The good things in your life are called blessings. Your family, friends, talents, even your favorite things— these are all blessings God has given you. But God doesn't want you to keep them all to yourself. He wants you to share!

If you know someone who seems lonely, invite him or her to be your friend. Ask your parents if you can have a friend over for dinner sometime. Give away some of your toys to kids who don't have very much. Sharing what God gave you is the best way to thank Him!

THOUGHT OF THE DAY

When you share God's blessings, they double!

PRAY TODAY

Dear God, thank You for all the blessings in my life! Please show me how I can share them with others. Amen.

WHAT WOULD JESUS DO?

Follow God's example, therefore, as dearly loved children.

EPHESIANS 5:1 NIV

None of us can be perfect like God. But we can all try to follow His example! One way to do this is to ask, "What would Jesus do?"

Jesus came to the world to show us how to live. He loved His mom and dad. He made good friends. He helped all sorts of people, and He was kind to everyone. He also didn't stay quiet when others were unkind—He stood up for what He knew was right. And most of all, He shared God's love with everyone. Jesus is the best example to follow!

THOUGHT OF THE DAY

If ever you don't have a clue, try asking, "What would Jesus do?"

PRAY TODAY

Dear God, thank You for sending Jesus! Help me do the things that He would do. Amen.

UNLIMITED CHANCES

Those who hide their sins won't succeed, but those who confess and give them up will receive mercy.

PROVERBS 28:13 CEB

You probably know it's best to tell the truth. But it's not always easy! When we've done something wrong, we may want to lie or just pretend it didn't happen. But when you tell God the truth, you never have to worry. God gives you unlimited chances to try again!

God will always forgive you. Then, He can help you ask others for forgiveness too. That's the best way to heal hurt feelings and make things right again. So never be afraid of telling the truth. God's forgiveness never runs out.

THOUGHT OF THE DAY

God will never not forgive. It's His favorite gift to give!

PRAY TODAY

Dear God, I'm so glad You will always forgive me. Please help me tell the truth—to You and others— even when it's hard. Amen.

@ @ @ @ @ @ @

HEAR AND DO

But be doers of the word and not hearers only.

JAMES 1:22A HCSB

B ible stories are pretty exciting! The Bible is full of interesting people, big adventures, and important lessons. It's so good to spend time hearing God's Word. But don't stop there!

God wants you to take what you know from the Bible and do something with it! Obey Jesus' directions to love everyone. Follow Ruth's example to work hard and help others. Listen to the story of the good Samaritan, and choose to be kind to people who are different from you. Don't just hear the Bible—do what it says!

THOUGHT OF THE DAY

What's a Bible story you love?

PRAY TODAY

Dear God, I love to listen to Bible stories. Please help me to be a doer, and not just a hearer! Amen.

TAKE GOOD CARE!

Don't you know that you are God's temple and that God's Spirit lives in you?

1 CORINTHIANS 3:16 NCV

One of God's greatest gifts is easy to see: your body! Your body lets you move around, see beautiful things, laugh big belly laughs, and enjoy yummy food. You and your body can do amazing things!

So how can you thank God for this super cool gift? Keep your body happy and healthy! Eat all kinds of good foods that help you grow. Take scrubby, bubbly baths, and brush your teeth every day. Wear a helmet when you ride your bike. You can do lots of things to care for the wonderful body God gave you!

THOUGHT OF THE DAY

What are three ways you can care for your body today?

PRAY TODAY

Dear God, thank You for giving me a body that can do so much! Help me take good care of it. Amen.

EVERYDAY ENCOURAGEMENT

You must encourage one another each day.

HEBREWS 3:13A CEV

Did you know you can do something every day that makes a big difference? You can be an encourager! Encouragement means helping others do or feel better. If a sibling is feeling sad, try telling them how much you love them. If a friend is trying to do something hard, you can say things like "I know you can do it!" And sometimes, all someone needs is a hug. Encouragement looks different ways at different times, and it doesn't cost a thing. So share some every day! Chances are, you'll feel great too.

THOUGHT OF THE DAY

See if you can encourage three people before lunch!

PRAY TODAY

Dear God, each day, please show me who needs encouragement and how I can help them. Amen.

GOD'S GOOD RULES

Through the Word we are put together and shaped up for the tasks God has for us.

2 TIMOTHY 3:17 MSG

Is it hard for you to follow the rules? Some people think rules are no fun. But God gave us good rules to show us how to be happy!

God gave Moses a list of simple instructions called the Ten Commandments. It's like a treasure map to a great life! When you follow the map, you'll live happily with your family and friends, and you'll have a strong friendship with God. Nothing could be better! So when you hear God telling you what to do, praise Him. He's showing you the way to the life He's planned for you.

THOUGHT OF THE DAY

God's rules totally rule!

PRAY TODAY

Dear God, sometimes it's hard to do what You want me to. Help me remember that You want what's best for me! Amen.

THINKING LIKE JESUS

Make your own attitude that of Christ Jesus.

PHILIPPIANS 2:5 HCSB

How you think is called your "attitude." If you choose to think angry or mean things, you will have a poor attitude. But if you choose to think like Jesus, you will have a great attitude.

How can you learn to think more like Jesus? When you hear Bible stories, pay attention to what Jesus did and said. He was kind. He helped others when they felt lonely or afraid. When you are at home or school, ask yourself "What would Jesus do or say?" Then do that! With practice you will soon have the same attitude as Jesus.

THOUGHT OF THE DAY

If you want to live the Jesus way, think "What would Jesus do or say?"

PRAY TODAY

Dear God, help me choose to have a good attitude, so that I can be more like Jesus every day. Amen.

HOW WOULD YOU FEEL?

For if you refuse to act kindly, you can hardly expect to be treated kindly. Kind mercy wins over harsh judgment every time.

JAMES 2:12–13 MSG

Has someone ever been mean to you? It feels pretty bad! Wouldn't you rather be treated kindly? Guess what? So would everyone else!

God wants us to have empathy—that means we should think about how our actions and words make other people feel. If it's hard to imagine someone else's feelings, ask yourself how YOU would feel. Then choose words that you would like to hear. When you are thoughtful about what you say and do, your kindness will probably be returned!

THOUGHT OF THE DAY

When in doubt, choose kindness over meanness every time.

PRAY TODAY

Dear God, please help me always to think before I speak. I like being treated with kindness, and I know others do too! Amen.

A ROYAL LAW

If you really keep the royal law according to the Scripture, "Love your neighbor as yourself," you are doing right.

JAMES 2:8 NIV

How do you like to be treated? Do you want others to say kind words? Share their toys? Invite you to play with them? Guess what? That's exactly how you should treat everyone else!

The Bible calls this idea the "royal law." That sounds pretty important! When you love others the same way you love yourself, you'll make them feel like kings and queens. And the best part is, you're showing them what God's love looks like too! So always try to remember the royal law. You'll be the queen of kindness!

THOUGHT OF THE DAY

The greatest way to wear a crown is spreading kindness in your town!

PRAY TODAY

Dear God, thank You for giving me such a great way to remember how to treat others. You are the real King of kindness! Amen.

A TINY SEED

"Truly I tell you, if you have faith as small as a mustard seed, you can say to this mountain, 'Move from here to there,' and it will move. Nothing will be impossible for you."

MATTHEW 17:20B NIV

Have you ever planted a seed? Seeds are usually very small. But when you plant them in good soil and give them water and sunlight, they can grow to become colorful flowers, tasty vegetables, or even huge trees!

God says that faith can grow too. Your faith can be as tiny as a seed—you don't have to know everything about God. But when you take care of your faith by reading your Bible, going to church, and praying, God will help your faith grow strong, just like a beautiful tree.

THOUGHT OF THE DAY

A tiny seed of faith can grow to do great things.

PRAY TODAY

Dear God, there is a lot I don't know, but I know I love You! Please help my seed of faith to grow big and strong. Amen.

KEEP BELIEVING

Immediately the father of the child cried out and said with tears, "Lord, I believe; help my unbelief!"

MARK 9:24 NKJV

Do you love to ask questions? God can handle any question you ask Him. And He never gets tired of them!

When you ask God questions, you show that you trust in His wisdom. So ask away! He may not answer quickly, and His answers may not always make sense to you right away. Try not to get discouraged. Keep asking God for help and believing in His goodness. And stay curious! When you stick close to God and talk to Him often, your faith gets stronger. Then you won't miss anything He has to say.

THOUGHT OF THE DAY

Sometimes answers show up in the Bible. Ask God to help you find them!

PRAY TODAY

Dear God, when I have a lot of questions, please help me trust You to give me the answers I need. Amen.

HOW WILL THEY KNOW?

"This is how everyone will recognize that you are my disciples—when they see the love you have for each other."

JOHN 13:35 MSG

God wants everyone to know you love Him. And do you know the best way to show that you love God? Love people!

Jesus says followers of God should be great at loving others. But not just when it's easy! Anyone can do that. Jesus wants you to love all the time. So ask for God's help. Look for ways to be kind and care for all people, no matter what they say or do. When you do that, everyone will see what God's love really looks like!

THOUGHT OF THE DAY

Can you think of someone who is hard to love? How can you love him or her today?

PRAY TODAY

Dear God, I want people to know how much I love You! Please help me show love to everyone I meet today. Amen.

PRAY FOR EVERYBODY

Hatred stirs up trouble, but love forgives all wrongs.

PROVERBS 10:12 NCV

If someone has hurt you, what should you do? God says you should pray for them! Why is that?

Sitting around feeling angry or annoyed only makes you feel more angry and annoyed. Nothing gets better! But saying a prayer for that person can help. That's because prayer is a loving action. So you have to put unhappy feelings aside—at least for a little while—when you pray.

Ask God to bless the person you're upset with and to forgive them for hurting you. Your prayer might be exactly what that person needs! And you'll feel better too.

THOUGHT OF THE DAY

Prayer changes things, starting with your own heart!

PRAY TODAY

Dear God, it can be hard to pray for people who have hurt me. Please give me a loving heart. Amen.

BRINGING JOY

And a voice from heaven said, "You are my dearly loved Son, and you bring me great joy."

MARK 1:11 NLT

The Bible tells us that Jesus gave God, His Father, great joy. You bring joy to your family too when you speak and act in ways that are good and right. Telling the truth, being kind to others, doing chores without complaining, looking for ways to help, and giving hugs are all simple ways you can show your love for your family.

And when you do these things, you are also bringing joy to God, your heavenly Father! Isn't it great to know that you can make others happy just like Jesus did?

THOUGHT OF THE DAY

What did you do this week to bring joy to the people around you?

PRAY TODAY

Dear God, please help me to be more like Jesus. I want to bring joy to my family. Amen.

THE GIFT OF WORDS

How wonderful it is to be able to say the right thing at the right time!

PROVERBS 15:23B TLB

It's fun to give a gift that you know someone will enjoy. And one of the best gifts you can give is a kind word!

You can do so much with kind words. You can cheer up someone who is feeling sad. You can ask questions that show a friend you care about her. You can share a silly joke, or help a younger sibling learn something new. You can encourage someone who is having a hard time. Gifts aren't always big, expensive, or sparkly. Most of the time, the right words mean more than anything you could buy at a store!

THOUGHT OF THE DAY

Who can you give a "word gift" to today? What will you say?

PRAY TODAY

Dear God, thank You for my friends and family. Please show me the right words to say to each of them every day! Amen.

READY TO RESIST

"Stay awake and pray for strength against temptation. The spirit wants to do what is right, but the body is weak."

MATTHEW 26:41 NCV

Everyone faces temptation now and then. Sometimes it's so hard to say no, even if you know something is wrong. What should you do when a friend starts to gossip or someone you admire asks you to break the rules?

Temptation can sneak up on you, so it's smart to have a plan. Talk to your parents about ways to stay strong when you feel tempted. Read your Bible, and learn how God helped others make good choices. Stay close to God, and you'll always be ready to resist!

THOUGHT OF THE DAY

Jesus used Bible verses to help Him fight temptation. Joseph simply ran away! What can you do?

PRAY TODAY

Dear God, You know what I need to say no to. Please give me strength and courage when I feel tempted! Amen.

@ @ @ @ @ @ @ @

THE BEST FRIENDS

Look for the best in each other, and always do your best to bring it out.

1 THESSALONIANS 5:15 MSG

What makes a good friend? It's nice when you enjoy the same things, or can make each other laugh. But the most important thing friends do is to help each other be their best.

That might mean helping them finish a hard job. Or being excited when they win a big soccer game! It might also mean encouraging them to make good choices, even when it's not easy. Everyone makes mistakes—even friends. Don't give up on them! When you forgive each other and find ways to be kind together, you can all be your very best!

THOUGHT OF THE DAY

If you want the best friends, BE a best friend! What can you do to help a friend today?

PRAY TODAY

Dear God, thank You for my friends! Please show me how to bring out the best in each one! Amen.

THINK BEFORE YOU SPEAK

A kind answer soothes angry feelings, but harsh words stir them up.

PROVERBS 15:1 CEV

Words are very powerful! They can encourage, or they can hurt feelings. So you have to be careful when you use them.

When you're angry, it's especially easy to say things you might feel bad about later. So take a deep breath and think carefully before you say anything. Try replacing any angry words with kind words instead. That will keep you from hurting anyone's feelings, and it could also help solve the problem. Wise King Solomon tells us that angry words only make an argument worse. So be part of the solution instead!

THOUGHT OF THE DAY

Practice kind responses so you can be ready for any conversation.

PRAY TODAY

Dear God, it's hard to think when I get angry. Help me pause and think before I speak. Amen.

A HAPPY HEART

Every day is hard for those who suffer, but a happy heart is like a continual feast.

PROVERBS 15:15 NCV

Have you ever noticed how some people always seem to complain about things? "This lunch looks yucky!" "I don't like this shirt." "My chores are too hard." "I never get what I want."

Maybe you also know some friends who always seem cheerful. "Hey, it's raining, but I love puddles!" "This isn't my favorite, but that's OK." "Here, you can have the bigger cookie!"

Which sounds better to you? Today's Bible verse says you'll have a lot more fun when you choose cheerfulness. So next time you feel like complaining, try saying something happy instead. Then see how it makes you feel!

THOUGHT OF THE DAY

Think of three things you're happy about today.

PRAY TODAY

Dear God, will You please help me to have a cheerful heart? I want to learn to look for ways to spread happiness. Amen.

KEEP ON GOING

But endurance must do its complete work, so that you may be mature and complete, lacking nothing.

JAMES 1:4 HCSB

Endurance is a long word that means "to keep on going." If you have endurance, you don't give up when things are hard. If you are learning to ride a bike, but you give up the first time you fall off, you'll never learn to ride. If you quit drawing pictures when they don't turn out the way you like, you won't learn how to draw better.

Endurance helps us become better at all sorts of things—from music to sports to friendships. It also helps us learn how to finish work that is hard. So ask God to help you endure. It's a gift worth working for!

THOUGHT OF THE DAY

What is a skill or task you need endurance to complete?

PRAY TODAY

Dear God, help me not to get discouraged when things don't work out the first time I try. Please help me to keep on going. Amen.

BE SMART AND WISE

Are there those among you who are truly wise and understanding? Then they should show it by living right and doing good things with a gentleness that comes from wisdom.

JAMES 3:13A NCV

Do you know the difference between being smart and being wise? Being smart means that you know things, like math, music, or spelling. Being wise means you use what you know to do what is right and good.

If you can solve math problems well, use that skill to help others. If you can play an instrument or sing, use your music to bring joy to someone. If you can write or draw well, create art that blesses others. Be creative! Ask God to help you find ways to be both smart AND wise.

THOUGHT OF THE DAY

How are you using something you know in a way that is wise?

PRAY TODAY

Dear God, thank You that I am learning so many new things. Please help me also learn how to be wise. Amen.

MANNERS MATTER

Let everyone see that you are considerate in all you do.

PHILIPPIANS 4:5A NLT

Here's an easy way to be kind: have good manners. Does that surprise you? It's true! When you're polite, you show others that you care about their feelings. And that makes them feel great!

Look for ways to practice good manners today. After you eat, you can take your empty plate to the kitchen. If you're at a restaurant, you can play quietly in your seat until everyone is ready to go. Join in conversations, and try not to interrupt others—even when you have something really fun to say! Good manners show others that they matter to you!

THOUGHT OF THE DAY

What manners are hardest for you to remember? What are the easiest?

PRAY TODAY

Dear God, thank You for giving me such a great way to show kindness! Please help me remember my manners every day. Amen.

@   @   @   @   @   @   @

ALWAYS THANKFUL

Give thanks to the LORD, for he is good! His faithful love endures forever.

PSALM 136:1 NLT

D o you write thank-you notes when you receive a present? A thank-you note shows someone that you appreciate a gift, and the time it took to send it!

You can send God thank-you notes too! Every day, God sends you good gifts. Did you have a fun time at school? Did you get to play with a good friend? Did you see a pretty butterfly or a silly squirrel? Even the love of your family and friends is a gift from God! So send Him a thank-you note today. You could make a pretty card or just say a prayer of thanks. God loves to know you appreciate His gifts!

THOUGHT OF THE DAY

What's something you can thank God for right now?

PRAY TODAY

Dear God, You have given me so many things. Please help me remember to say thank You! Amen.

GOD'S GREAT POWER

I pray . . . that you may know . . . incomparably great power for us who believe.

EPHESIANS 1:18–19 NIV

Have you ever wished that you could have a superhero by your side? Would it make you feel stronger or braver? Well, here's a secret: you do! You have God with you, and He is stronger and more powerful than any superhero you can imagine!

Nothing can make God stop loving you. No power on earth or in the heavens is greater than God. He made every star, and He keeps the planets in their places. He can help you solve any problem, and He can help you face any fear. God will never fail you!

THOUGHT OF THE DAY

God's power keeps you in His care, and He goes with you everywhere!

PRAY TODAY

Dear God, You are more powerful than any superhero. Thank You for loving me and taking care of me. Amen.

THE GIFT OF GUIDES

Remember what you are taught. And listen carefully to words of knowledge.

PROVERBS 23:12 ICB

God wants us to learn good lessons. So He puts people in our lives who can share their wisdom and experience to help us make good choices.

You probably have good teachers and pastors you like. Or maybe your grandparents give you great advice. And of course, your parents have lots of lessons to teach you! Think of these people as God-given guides. The words they say and the stories they share can help you live your very best life. So pay attention! You never know what God wants you to learn next.

THOUGHT OF THE DAY

What are some good lessons your parents have taught you?

PRAY TODAY

Dear God, thank You for all the great guides in my life. Help me listen carefully and learn well! Amen.

LAUGH TOGETHER

How we laughed and sang for joy. And the other nations said, "What amazing things the Lord has done for them."

PSALM 126:2 TLB

Have you ever been so happy you can't stop laughing? Sometimes a joke gives us the giggles. Sometimes a silly song or a goofy game will get you chuckling. Laughing can make a bad day good, and a good day even better!

God loves to hear us laugh. But it's a good idea to make sure everyone else is laughing too. If someone is left out or has hurt feelings, that's not very funny. It's never OK to laugh at someone. Instead, laugh with them! Find something that everyone agrees is silly. Then enjoy a good laugh, and a happy heart.

THOUGHT OF THE DAY

Larry loves to sing silly songs. Can you make up a silly song?

PRAY TODAY

Dear God, thank You for the gift of funny, happy times with my friends and family. What makes You laugh? Amen.

GOD'S BLESSINGS

You are wonderful . . . you store up blessings for all who honor and trust you.

PSALM 31:19 CEV

God is so good that He loves to give blessings to all of us. Blessings are wonderful gifts that only God can give. He gives us His words in the Bible so we can know Him and know how to live. He gives us friends and family so we can understand love and friendship. He gives us minds so we can think and learn and imagine. He gives us all these amazing things now, and He says that He has even more blessings stored up for us in heaven! Isn't that wonderful news?

THOUGHT OF THE DAY

Name some of the blessings you want to thank God for today!

PRAY TODAY

Dear God, thank You for all of the blessings You have given me. Help me always remember them. Amen.

TRACKING JESUS

For God called you to do good, even if it means suffering, just as Christ suffered for you. He is your example, and you must follow in his steps.

1 PETER 2:21 NLT

Some people know how to follow animals in the woods by "tracking" them. They understand how different animals act and can even find their footprints (or pawprints!) to figure out where they've been.

The Bible tells us to follow Jesus' steps. We can't see them like footprints, but we can get to know Jesus so well that we understand His ways. When you read Bible stories, think of what Jesus is like. How does He treat people? What's important to Him? Then look for ways to be more like Him. That's how you follow Jesus!

THOUGHT OF THE DAY

Get better at "tracking" Jesus by reading about Him in the Bible.

PRAY TODAY

Dear God, I want to follow Jesus. Any time I have a choice to make, help me imagine what Jesus would do! Amen.

SONGS FOR GOD

Sing to the LORD a new song; sing to the LORD, all the earth. Sing to the LORD and praise his name; every day tell how he saves us.

PSALM 96:1–2 NCV

The Bible is full of songs. Miriam sang to God after her brother Moses led the Israelites safely out of Egypt. Mary sang a song when she learned she would be Jesus' mother. And King David wrote many songs for God in the book of Psalms!

You can sing to God any time you want. Praise Him for all the great things He does! Sing a song to share your thoughts or even ask for help. Whether it's a favorite song from church or a song you just made up, sing it loud and proud. God loves to hear your voice!

THOUGHT OF THE DAY
Try adding a song to your prayers tonight!

PRAY TODAY
Dear God, sometimes I feel so happy, I just have to sing! Thank You for creating music so I can sing to You. Amen.

LEARN FROM YOUR MISTAKES

No one in this world always does right.

ECCLESIASTES 7:20 CEV

Nobody does everything right all the time. It isn't always easy to follow the rules in a new place or keep your temper or tell the truth. But here's some very good news: God is ready to forgive you and to help you learn from all of your mistakes! How did your actions or words make you feel? Do you need to apologize to someone? What can you do differently next time? A mistake is a perfect chance to keep growing into the person God wants you to be!

THOUGHT OF THE DAY

Everyone makes mistakes. But not everyone learns from them. Be sure you do!

PRAY TODAY

Dear God, sometimes it's hard for me to make good choices. Please help me learn from my mistakes! Amen.

FORGIVENESS STARTS WITH YOU

But if we confess our sins to God, he can always be trusted to forgive us and take our sins away.

1 JOHN 1:9 CEV

We know that it's important to forgive others. But did you know it's also important to forgive yourself? It's true! Everyone makes mistakes and wrong choices. Try not to get too frustrated. The important thing is to learn from your mistakes and ask God to help you try again next time.

God doesn't expect you to be perfect. He expects you to try your best and admit when you're wrong. Remember that He loves you, and He's promised to forgive you no matter what. So trust Him and forgive yourself too!

THOUGHT OF THE DAY

No one is perfect. Everyone needs God!

PRAY TODAY

Dear God, thank You for loving me. Help me show myself kindness and forgiveness when I make mistakes. Amen.

POWERFUL WORDS

Be gracious in your speech. The goal is to bring out the best in others in a conversation, not put them down, not cut them out.

COLOSSIANS 4:6 MSG

What can you do with words? You can tell a joke, share an idea, ask a question, or calm someone down. Words can be really helpful! But if you're not careful, words can also hurt. They are powerful tools, and God wants you to choose them carefully.

So when you speak, ask yourself, "Will the things I say show God's love?" Gossip and unkind words make others feel angry or sad. But encouragement shows others that they are valuable and important. That's how God wants everyone to feel. So use your powerful words for good!

THOUGHT OF THE DAY

When kindness shines through every word, God is pleased with what He's heard!

PRAY TODAY

Dear God, I know that words have power. Help me use that power to share Your love with everyone! Amen.

@ @ @ @ @ @ @

BE GENEROUS!

"It is more blessed to give than to receive."

ACTS 20:35 ESV

It's fun to get gifts or hear kind words. But it's also fun to give those things to others. In fact, it can be even better!

When you give to others, that's called being generous. God wants us to be generous with all the good gifts He's given us. How can you be generous? Some people need help to get food or clothes, so you could donate to a food bank or a shelter. Some people need you to share friendship with them. Try inviting someone new to play with your friends. You may find that giving feels even better than getting, because it means twice as much joy!

THOUGHT OF THE DAY

Be generous with kindness today. Draw a picture to give to someone special!

PRAY TODAY

Dear God, You have given me great gifts! Help me to be generous and share them with others. Amen.

PEACE THAT LASTS

"You keep him in perfect peace whose mind is stayed on you, because he trusts in you."

ISAIAH 26:3 ESV

Do you ever have a hard time feeling peaceful? It's not always easy! But God offers peace that sticks around. All you have to do is trust Him.

God loves you. He knows everything, and He has good plans for you! He has promised He'll never leave, no matter what happens. So when you trust God, you don't have to worry about anything! Instead, you can feel peaceful, because you know God has everything under control. What could be better than that?

THOUGHT OF THE DAY

God's peace isn't hard to find. Just keep Him always on your mind!

PRAY TODAY

Dear God, thank You that I can find peace in You, no matter what happens! Amen.

e ⊚ e ⊚ ⊚ e e ⊚

HOME SWEET HOME

"If a kingdom is divided against itself, that kingdom cannot stand. If a house is divided against itself, that house cannot stand."

MARK 3:24–25 NIV

Who lives with you in your home? Mom and Dad? Brothers and sisters? Grandparents or aunts and uncles? Family is one of God's most special gifts, and when everyone cares for each other, home is a fun and happy place!

Sometimes you might feel annoyed with someone in your family. That's normal! The important thing is to choose kind words, find ways to solve problems together, and apologize for hurt feelings right away. That way, everyone feels loved, safe, and supported. It's the kind of home God wants all of us to have!

THOUGHT OF THE DAY

How does your home make you feel?

PRAY TODAY

Dear God, thank You for my family. Please help us have fun and care for each other, even when we disagree! Amen.

GOD HOLDS YOUR HAND

"Don't be afraid, for I am with you. Don't be discouraged, for I am your God. I will strengthen you and help you. I will hold you up with my victorious right hand."

ISAIAH 41:10 NLT

Have you ever been afraid to do something? Maybe you had to walk into a new school or class. Or maybe you had to try something you'd never done before. If you are afraid, isn't it great to have someone go with you and hold your hand?

God says that He wants to help you whenever you feel afraid. Even though you can't see Him, He is always there, just like a best friend. You can imagine God holding your hand in His and walking with you when you're afraid. He will give you strength and courage because He loves you!

THOUGHT OF THE DAY

There's nothing to fear when you know God is near!

PRAY TODAY

Dear God, thank You for holding my hand and helping me be strong and brave. Amen.

SHOWING LOVE

Little children, let us stop just saying we love people; let us really love them, and show it by our actions.

1 JOHN 3:18 TLB

Did you know you can show people you love them without even using words? You can color a picture and give it to someone. You can help your siblings do their chores. You can give your mom a hug. There are so many ways to say "I love you" without saying a thing! The Bible says the best way to tell people you love them is to act with love and kindness. Can you think of ways to say "I love you" without saying a single word?

THOUGHT OF THE DAY

The very best way to say "I love you" is not with words, but with what you do!

PRAY TODAY

Dear God, please help me show Your love to others by using actions as well as words! Amen.

GROW IN GRACE

But grow in the grace and knowledge of our Lord and Savior Jesus Christ. To Him be the glory both now and forever. Amen.

2 PETER 3:18 NKJV

You know what it means to grow tall and strong. But God also wants us to grow in knowledge and grace. What does that mean?

You can grow in knowledge by learning new things. Listen to your Sunday school teacher, memorize verses, and read Bible stories at home to get to know God better. You can grow in grace by doing what God says and trusting that He loves you. The cool thing is that as you learn more about God, it gets easier to follow and trust Him. So you actually grow in knowledge and grace at the same time!

THOUGHT OF THE DAY

Pick a time each day to read your Bible.

PRAY TODAY

Dear God, thank You for Your love. Please help me grow in knowledge and grace every single day! Amen.

BEING COURTEOUS

. . . to speak evil of no one, to avoid quarreling, to be gentle, and to show perfect courtesy toward all people.

TITUS 3:2 ESV

Being courteous means using good manners and showing kindness to others. There are many ways to show courtesy at home and at school. Using words like "please" and "thank you" and saying "I'm sorry" or "excuse me" are all ways to be courteous and kind. You can also listen patiently when others are talking and take turns when you're playing. These words and actions help us all get along together. They are ways to show we care about other people like God wants us to. Look for ways to be courteous today!

THOUGHT OF THE DAY

Saying "thanks" and "please" will help to put a friend at ease.

PRAY TODAY

Dear God, please help me to always treat others with courtesy and kindness. Amen.

LIVING IN LOVE

We know how much God loves us, and we have put our trust in his love. God is love, and all who live in love live in God, and God lives in them.

1 JOHN 4:16 NLT

How can you know God better? You can read your Bible and go to church. You can pray and spend time with Him! But don't forget one of the best ways to know God: live in love!

Living in love means that everything you do or say comes from a loving heart. Doing your chores without complaining is a good way to live in love. So is sharing your toys or standing up for someone who is being teased or left out. When you choose to act lovingly, you are growing closer to God. That's because God IS love!

THOUGHT OF THE DAY

You can love others best when you think about how much God loves YOU!

PRAY TODAY

Dear God, thank You for loving me so much. Please help me do everything with a loving heart. Amen.

YOU HAVE SO MUCH!

"I came that they may have and enjoy life, and have it in abundance [to the full, till it overflows]."

JOHN 10:10 AMP

When you follow Jesus, your life is full! That doesn't mean it's full of things. You might not get every toy you want or go on every cool vacation your friends do. But you get to fill your days with wonderful gifts from God!

When you try something new, you have confidence God will help you. When you feel afraid, you have peace that God is there. You can get excited about tomorrow because God has great plans for you! You can celebrate today because He loves you with a huge love. What a great big life you have with Jesus!

THOUGHT OF THE DAY

What are some things you enjoy about your life?

PRAY TODAY

Dear God, thank You for my big life! You have given me such wonderful gifts! Amen.

MAKING CHOICES

I am offering you life or death, blessings or curses. Now, choose life! . . . To choose life is to love the L ORD your God, obey him, and stay close to him.

DEUTERONOMY 30:19-20 NCV

How do you make a choice? Do you pick the petals off a daisy? Do you flip a coin? Do you ask someone to pick a hand? Did you know there is a much better way to make a choice?

The Bible says that when we love God, obey Him, and stay close to Him, He helps us make good decisions. We can stay close to God by reading His words in the Bible and by talking to Him in prayer. Then, when those tough choices come along, He'll show us the right thing to do!

THOUGHT OF THE DAY

Next time you have to make a tough choice, talk to God first. He loves to help!

PRAY TODAY

Dear God, every day is filled with choices. Will You please help me make good ones? Amen.

SPEAKING COURAGEOUSLY

"Be strong! Be courageous! Do not be afraid of them! For the Lord your God will be with you. He will neither fail you nor forsake you."

DEUTERONOMY 31:6 TLB

The Bible tells a lot of stories about prophets. Prophets are men and women who told others about God. Sometimes people didn't believe the prophets or tried to hurt them. But God gave each prophet courage to tell the truth and do the right thing. Because of brave prophets, lots of people heard about God's love and came to believe in Him.

You might meet people who don't believe in God like you do. Ask God to give you courage to share the good news about His love. You can be just like the brave prophets in the Bible!

THOUGHT OF THE DAY
Have you ever shared God's love with someone new?

PRAY TODAY
Dear God, please give me courage to tell everyone about Your love! Amen.

RESPECTFUL ACTIONS

Being respected is more important than having great riches.

PROVERBS 22:1 ICB

When you treat people with respect, you show them that they are valuable. In fact, the Bible says that respect is a better gift than riches!

Being polite is an excellent way to treat others with respect. Always share, say "please" and "thank you," and try not to interrupt when someone is talking. If your mom or dad or a teacher asks you to do something, do it right away instead of complaining. Say a kind word to someone, or just hold the door open for the person behind you. Even the smallest respectful action can make someone's day!

THOUGHT OF THE DAY

Choose a specific way to show respect to five people today.

PRAY TODAY

Dear God, I want to be respectful. Please help me treat everyone I meet with respect. Amen.

@ @ @ @ @ @ @

GOD KNOWS YOUR NEEDS

And my God will supply every need of yours according to his riches in glory in Christ Jesus.

PHILIPPIANS 4:19 ESV

The Bible says that God will give His children everything they need. Sometimes people think that means that God will give them everything they want—like the newest toys, games, or clothes. Those things are fun to have, but the gifts God gives us are much more wonderful.

God gives us His love, peace, and joy. He blesses us with friends and family. He always listens to our prayers, and He's made big plans for us. God doesn't promise to give us everything we want, but He does provide everything we need. Be sure to tell God "thanks" today!

THOUGHT OF THE DAY

God always provides His best for His children.

PRAY TODAY

Dear God, thank You for loving me and providing all I need. Amen.

JUST AS YOU ARE

But God showed how much he loved us by having Christ die for us, even though we were sinful.

ROMANS 5:8 CEV

Jesus loves you just as you are. So don't worry about being perfect. No one is! You'll make mistakes and wrong choices, but Jesus' love will never change. He will never leave you, and He'll never stop listening to your prayers.

In fact, Jesus loves you so much that He gave His life so you could live with Him forever in heaven! All you have to do is say yes to His love. And when you say yes to Jesus, He'll show you how to share His love with others too. Since nobody's perfect, everyone needs Jesus' love.

THOUGHT OF THE DAY

Jesus lived a perfect life so we don't have to!

PRAY TODAY

Dear Jesus, thank You for loving me enough to give Your life for me. I know I'm not perfect— and I'm glad I don't need to be! Amen.

SUPER POWER

Do not withhold good from those who deserve it when it's in your power to help them.

PROVERBS 3:27 NLT

Superheroes have many different powers. Some are very strong. Some can fly. Some can become invisible! But do you know that you have a special superpower too? The Bible says that you have the power to do something good for someone who needs help!

Whom do you know who could use some help today? Does your sister or brother need help learning something new? Does your mom or dad need you to help by doing your chores with a smile? Ask God to give you some ideas. Then use your superpower to help others today!

If you see a need, don't wait to be asked. Jump right in! That's how to be a superhero for God!

THOUGHT OF THE DAY

What can you do to help a friend or family member today?

PRAY TODAY

Dear God, thank You for giving me the superpower to be a great helper! Amen.

FOOLISH FIGHTERS

It's a mark of good character to avert quarrels, but fools love to pick fights.

PROVERBS 20:3 MSG

When you and a friend or family member disagree, what do you do? Some people love to argue, say mean things, or even hit each other! Did you know that the Bible says those people are fools?

When you disagree with someone, don't be a fool. Look for ways to solve your disagreements without fighting. Maybe you can take turns. Or maybe you can take a break from being around each other and then come back and try again later. Fighting never ends up well. Good friends don't want to hurt one another. They want to find peaceful solutions, then get back to having fun!

THOUGHT OF THE DAY

What are some ways you can keep from fighting with others?

PRAY TODAY

Dear God, when I feel like fighting, help me remember to think about what You would want me to do instead. Amen.

SHINE YOUR LIGHT

"You are the light of the world. A city situated on a hill cannot be hidden."

MATTHEW 5:14 HCSB

Did you know that people pay attention to what you do and say? Just like a light on a hilltop shows people where the hill is, the way you act shows others where your heart is. If you are being kind, helping, playing fair, and telling the truth, others notice. They know your heart is in the right place.

Being a good example is like shining a light for Jesus. He wants you to show others the right way to live, speak, and act. When others see your light, they can follow you to Him. So be a light wherever you go!

THOUGHT OF THE DAY

Don't forget to shine your light by doing and saying what is right!

PRAY TODAY

Dear God, I want others to see Jesus shining in me. Please help me to do and say good things. Amen.

YOU'RE SO VERY SPECIAL

"I have loved you with a love that lasts forever. I have kept on loving you with a kindness that never fails."

JEREMIAH 31:3B NIRV

No one else in the entire world is exactly like you. God made you to have a unique set of talents, ideas, feelings, and thoughts. The world needs you to be you!

You might have days when you wish you could be like someone else. Of course, you can learn from people you admire, like teachers, leaders, and your parents. But remember that you are important to God because of who YOU are. If you ever feel like you're not special, just talk to God. He can't wait to show you how amazing and wonderful you truly are.

THOUGHT OF THE DAY

Can you think of three things that make you special and unique?

PRAY TODAY

Dear God, thank You for making me the way I am. Help me remember that I am very important to You! Amen.

@ @ @ @ @ @ @

PATIENT AND KIND

Love is patient; love is kind.

1 CORINTHIANS 13:4 HCSB

When is it easy to be kind? Probably when you feel happy, right? When you're playing with a friend or making cookies with Mom, kind words come quickly. But what about when someone at school hurts your feelings, or your little brother or sister interrupts your favorite show? You might feel like saying unkind words instead!

God asks us to show love all the time. That means choosing kindness, especially when it's hard. It takes extra patience to be kind when you're frustrated, but take a breath and ask God for help. He can give you the best words to say!

THOUGHT OF THE DAY

Kindness doesn't mean you ignore how you feel. Just try explaining your feelings calmly and patiently!

PRAY TODAY

Dear God, I'm glad Your love is both patient and kind. Help me show that kind of love to everyone in my life. Amen.

JUST CELEBRATE!

Celebrate God all day, every day.

PHILIPPIANS 4:4 MSG

Are you ready to party? The Bible tells us that we can celebrate every single day! That's because God is good, and He loves us no matter what. What could be better than that?

Think of all the things that make you smile! Do you have good friends? Did you have fun with your family today? Maybe the sun is shining brightly right now, or the rain is giving the garden a good drink. Every day is filled with reasons to praise God. So sing a song or jump for joy! God loves to see you celebrate!

THOUGHT OF THE DAY

How would you throw a party for God?

PRAY TODAY

Dear God, You are amazing! Help me remember to celebrate You every single day! Amen.

CHOOSING WISDOM

Wisdom is more precious than rubies. Nothing you could want is equal to it.

PROVERBS 8:11 NCV

If you could have anything in the world, what would you choose? When God asked King Solomon to choose whatever he wanted, he chose wisdom. That might seem strange, but Solomon knew that if he had all the money or fame in the world, but he wasn't wise, he would lose everything.

God says that we can have wisdom too! All we have to do is ask for it. The next time you have to make a hard choice, ask God to give you wisdom to choose what's best. He promises that He will!

THOUGHT OF THE DAY

What was a time when you had to make a hard choice? How did God help you?

PRAY TODAY

Dear God, thank You for offering me the gift of wisdom. Help me remember to ask You whenever I have to make a hard choice. Amen.

A SERVING SUPERHERO!

". . . I tell you the truth, anything you did for even the least of my people here, you also did for me."

MATTHEW 25:40 NCV

Larryboy may be a pretty silly looking superhero, but one thing's for sure: he always tries to help others! You don't need a cape and a funny hat to be a hero. Just look for ways to serve the people around you.

Is your dad busy making dinner? Swoop in and set the table without being asked! Does your mom need help with a big pile of laundry? Fly over and fold along with her! Hurry in to hold the door for someone, or rescue a friend by reminding her how special she is. There are so many ways to help people. How will you be a hero today?

THOUGHT OF THE DAY

Can you surprise someone with service today? Get creative and have fun!

PRAY TODAY

Dear God, please show me how I can help those around me. I want to be a Serving Superhero! Amen.

GETTING TO KNOW HIM

Yes, it is through Christ we all have the right to come to the Father in one Spirit.

EPHESIANS 2:18 NCV

Have you ever wondered what God is really like? Here's a clue: look at Jesus! The Bible says Jesus is the key to understanding who God is.

Think about your favorite stories of Jesus. How does He treat people? What does He care about? Those are the things that are important to God. Jesus loves people unconditionally—that means "no matter what." That's how God loves each of us. So invite Jesus to live in your heart today. When you get to know Jesus, you get to know God!

THOUGHT OF THE DAY

What's your favorite story about Jesus?

PRAY TODAY

Dear God, thank You for sending Jesus so I can understand You better! Amen.

WHAT'S IN YOUR FUTURE?

We can make our plans, but the LORD determines our steps.

PROVERBS 16:9 NLT

I s there something you want to do when you grow up? Isn't it fun to have dreams? God has a dream for your future too! And He wants to help you make it come true.

God's dreams and your dreams might be the same, or they might not. If things don't go exactly the way you expect, don't worry! Remember that God is taking care of you and His plans are very good.

No one knows what the future will bring. Keep dreaming along with God, and see where He takes you!

THOUGHT OF THE DAY

Trust God with your present, and He will make your future bright.

PRAY TODAY

Dear God, thank You for planning so many good things for my future! Help me trust You with all my dreams. Amen.

A GOOD WORK IN YOU

God began doing a good work in you, and I am sure he will continue it until it is finished when Jesus Christ comes again.

PHILIPPIANS 1:6 NCV

God loves you so much. He worked hard to make you just the way you are. And He is working hard to help you grow each day. He has wonderful plans for you! You are God's treasure. So remember to treat yourself with love and respect! It's normal to feel frustrated when you make a mistake. Or to get upset when you're learning something new. But try to be patient and forgive yourself. There is good work happening inside you, even if you don't feel that way! God won't ever give up—and neither should you!

THOUGHT OF THE DAY

What are some things you are learning?

PRAY TODAY

Dear God, thank You for working so hard to make me special. Please help me to be kind to myself! Amen.

YOUR VERY BEST FRIEND

Jesus Christ is the same yesterday and today and forever.

HEBREWS 13:8 ESV

D o you have some really good friends? Good friends are people you can count on to do what they say. And they always take care of each other!

When you ask Jesus to come live in your heart, He becomes your best friend. You can tell Him whatever you're thinking about, and He promises to care for you and help you. If you make a wrong choice or a big mistake, you never have to worry! Jesus will always love and forgive you. In fact, with Jesus, you not only get a best friend—you get a forever friend!

THOUGHT OF THE DAY

Who are some of your good friends? How do you show each other you care?

PRAY TODAY

Dear Jesus, thank You for being my very best friend! I'm so glad we're friends forever. Amen.

PRAY ABOUT IT!

"The eyes of the LORD watch over those who do right, and his hears are open to their prayers."

1 PETER 3:12 NLT

Did you know that you have a secret tool you can use any time, day or night? Prayer! You can pray about anything any time you want. Do you want to get better at something? Pray for God's help. Is something bothering you? Pray for God's comfort. Are you nervous about meeting someone new? Pray for God's peace. Anything you want to pray about, God is ready to listen. He loves for you to share your heart with Him, and He can always help you. So don't waste time worrying about anything. Pray right away!

THOUGHT OF THE DAY

Prayer changes things. Try it and see!

PRAY TODAY

Dear God, thank You for always being there to listen when I pray. Help me remember to talk to You when I'm worried. Amen.

WHAT DOES GOD SEE?

Create in me a pure heart, God, and make my spirit right again.

PSALM 51:10 NCV

When we disobey God, we might feel yucky inside. But God can fix that! You can tell God what went wrong, and then ask Him to help you try again. It feels great when God sets things right in your heart.

God loves to see you make good choices. But He also knows that everyone makes mistakes. When you ask God for forgiveness, He is so excited! That shows you love Him and want to follow Him. God always forgives when you ask. Then He can help you grow in kindness, wisdom, and love.

THOUGHT OF THE DAY

Any time your heart feels sad, God can clean it and make you glad!

PRAY TODAY

Dear God, thank You for loving me, inside and out! Please help me keep a clean heart. Amen.

PATIENCE FOR ALL

Be gentle to everyone, able to teach, and patient.

2 TIMOTHY 2:24B HCSB

Has someone ever told you to be patient? Sometimes patience means waiting to do something that you want to do. But sometimes patience means taking your time and choosing gentleness. Being patient is one of the best ways to show God's love.

When you help a younger sibling learn something new, that's a great chance to be patient. When you get upset, but you choose kind words instead of angry actions, you're showing gentleness. And every time you put someone else first, you're sharing God's great love! How can you practice patience today?

THOUGHT OF THE DAY

Patience takes practice, and practice makes perfect!

PRAY TODAY

Dear God, it's not always easy to be patient. Please help me practice, so I can share Your love! Amen.

WORSHIPPING GOD

Oh come, let us worship and bow down; let us kneel before the LORD, our Maker!

PSALM 95:6 ESV

The Bible tells us to worship God because He is the One who made us. He is a mighty King!

There are many ways we can show that we love and respect God. We can kneel or bow our heads when we pray. We can sing and raise our hands to Him in joy and thanks! We can obey His words in the Bible. Just think about how amazing God is and about all the wonderful things He has made! He totally deserves all of our praise and worship. So raise your voice or bow your head or start dancing! God is great!

THOUGHT OF THE DAY

How do you want to worship God today?

PRAY TODAY

Dear God, You are greater than anything I can understand. Today I will choose to worship and praise You. Amen.

FAMILY HARMONY

And above all these put on love, which binds everything together in perfect harmony.

COLOSSIANS 3:14 ESV

Have you ever heard a band play music? The different instruments each look and sound different. A tuba is big and makes a low sound. A flute is long and thin and makes high notes. The drums say "boom, boom, boom" or "rat-a-tat-tat." But when they all play together they make wonderful music. That's called harmony.

In a family, each person has different feelings and does different things. But when everyone in a family works together with love, they live together in perfect harmony, just like an awesome band! And that's exactly how God wants us to live.

THOUGHT OF THE DAY

What part do you play in your family?

PRAY TODAY

Dear God, thank You for my family. We are not all the same, so we need Your love to help us make beautiful harmony together. Amen.

GOD'S RULES

Practice God's law—get a reputation for wisdom.

PROVERBS 28:7 MSG

Do you have rules to follow at home? Maybe you have to go to bed at a certain time or set the table each night. And I'll bet you aren't allowed to kick or hit! Rules at home help keep everyone safe and happy.

God has also made rules that will keep you safe and happy. And just like rules at home, it takes practice to follow them well. What matters most to God is that you try. So if you make a mistake, just talk to God about what you can do differently next time. Then try again!

THOUGHT OF THE DAY

When you work to learn God's way, you'll get better every day!

PRAY TODAY

Dear God, thank You for helping me try again whenever I need to. I want to learn to follow all Your good rules! Amen.

HOW TO BE A GOOD FRIEND

My dear, dear friends, if God loved us like this, we certainly ought to love each other.

1 JOHN 4:11 MSG

God wants us to love our friends just like He loves us. That's a pretty strong love! What do you think that would look like?

God listens to our prayers, so we should listen when our friends share stories or ask for help. God cares for us, so we should take care of our friends and show them love. And most importantly, God always works for our good. So look for ways to build your friends up! When you do these things, you'll become better friends with everyone—including God!

THOUGHT OF THE DAY

God rejoices over us, so we should rejoice over each other! Thank God for your friends today.

PRAY TODAY

Dear God, thank You for my friends! We all have so much fun. Help me to be the very best friend I can be. Amen.

GOD'S HELPING HANDS

Now the God of all grace, who called you to His eternal glory in Christ Jesus, will personally restore, establish, strengthen, and support you.

1 PETER 5:10 HCSB

God is the greatest Helper there is. No matter what problem you're facing, God will guide you through. When things get tough, God is stronger. When you feel sad, God will comfort you. And when you feel happy, God will celebrate with you!

God's love never ends, and neither does His help. He never gets tired or distracted. Your life is His greatest joy, and He loves to share it with you! He is all around you, all the time. So take His hand and follow His lead. He's here to help.

THOUGHT OF THE DAY
Trust God and watch what He can do!

PRAY TODAY
Dear God, thank You for Your always-there, never-failing helping hands! I love knowing I can count on You. Amen.

THINK FIRST!

Enthusiasm without knowledge is not good. If you act too quickly, you might make a mistake.

PROVERBS 19:2 NCV

God loves for you to enjoy every day. He wants you to have a great time learning and growing and trying new things!

It's good to get excited. It's OK to have big feelings. But those are times it's easy to act too quickly and make mistakes. God says slowing down can help. Try thinking about what can happen next. If you grab a toy away from your little sister, how will she feel? If you run outside in the snow without a coat, will you be comfortable? Thinking first is always the best choice!

THOUGHT OF THE DAY

When you think before you act, you'll have more fun. Now that's a fact!

PRAY TODAY

Dear God, it's hard to slow down when I feel excited or upset. Will You please help me to think before I act and speak? Amen.

SOMETHING GOOD

And we know that for those who love God all things work together for good, for those who are called according to his purpose.

ROMANS 8:28 ESV

Have you ever made a mistake when drawing a picture? Did you ever build something and then it broke? Sometimes when we make mistakes or ruin something, we just toss it out. But God says even when we make mistakes or feel like we have done something wrong He will never give up on us! He will always love us. God can even take our mistakes and make something good out of them. He will never give up on us, and He loves to surprise us with blessings. What a wonderful God!

THOUGHT OF THE DAY

Look for ways God is making something good in your life today!

PRAY TODAY

Dear God, I don't understand why things go wrong sometimes, but I am so glad You can make anything into something good. Amen.

VISITING GOD'S HOUSE

"For where two or three are gathered together in My name, I am there among them."

MATTHEW 18:20 HCSB

Some churches are big. Others are small. Some churches are in the city. Some are in the country. Wherever your church is, God says He is there. That's because a church is not just a building—it is God's house! And just like you like to have friends come over, God loves when you visit His house. He loves to hear you sing and talk to Him, and He wants you to know that you are loved.

The next time you go to church or Sunday school, remember that you are visiting God at His house! You are always a welcomed guest and friend.

THOUGHT OF THE DAY

What are some things you like to do at God's house?

PRAY TODAY

Dear God, thanks for loving me and inviting me to Your house. Amen.

ONE STEP AT A TIME

All things should be done in the right way, one after the other.

1 CORINTHIANS 14:40 NLV

Sometimes, we all have to do things we don't like. It's easy to put off difficult or boring work until another day. But God can help us do what needs to be done, one step at a time.

Try to break a big (or boring) job into little pieces. Giving the dog a bath seems like a lot of work! But think about it in smaller steps like filling the tub, getting a towel, making soap bubbles, scrubbing your dog's belly, and cozy cuddles afterward! You only need to do one step at a time. Pretty soon, your work will be done!

THOUGHT OF THE DAY

When something hard needs to get done, smaller steps can make it fun!

PRAY TODAY

Dear God, when I have a big job to do, please help me find ways to make it seem easy and fun! Amen.

SURPRISE THEM!

Don't repay evil for evil. Don't retaliate with insults when people insult you. Instead, pay them back with a blessing.

1 PETER 3:9A NLT

When someone is kind to you, it's easy to be kind in return. But what about when someone says something mean, or does something you don't like? Should you be mean back?

No! In fact, God says you should surprise them with kindness! If they use hurtful words, find helpful words to say. If someone takes something away from you, don't take something in return. And remember to pray for them later! When you choose gentleness instead of anger, God will bless you with peace and joy. And maybe even a new friend! What a great surprise!

THOUGHT OF THE DAY

Maybe someone just needs help being kind. You can lead the way!

PRAY TODAY

Dear God, please show me how to surprise others with blessings today. Amen.

TALKING TO GOD

Be gracious to me, Lord, for I call to You all day long.

PSALM 86:3 HCSB

Even though you cannot see God, He wants you to know He is always with you. When you spend time praying, singing, or even thinking about God, He hears you and it makes Him glad.

Reading Bible stories or devotional books like this one help you to know God better. You can talk to God anytime—and all the time! He wants to hear from you and promises to help you. It doesn't matter where you are or what you are doing, God is always there to guide you. He loves you more than you can imagine!

THOUGHT OF THE DAY

When do you like to talk to God?

PRAY TODAY

Dear God, I'm so glad I can talk to You anytime. Thank You for always being there for me. Amen.

WHAT ARE YOU DOING?

Here's what you do: Live well, live wisely, live humbly. It's the way you live, not the way you talk, that counts.

JAMES 3:13B MSG

Have you ever heard the expression, "Actions speak louder than words"? What that means is that what we do tells people more about us than what we say. If you say you play fair, but then you cheat at a game, what do your actions say about you? If you make a promise, but then you break it, will people believe what you say?

Our words are important, but our actions are even more important. Show everyone the kind of person you are by doing what is right and treating others with kindness. That's the wise way to live.

THOUGHT OF THE DAY

Let your actions show others that you belong to Jesus.

PRAY TODAY

Dear God, I want to please You by what I do and say. Please help me to show others that I am Your child. Amen.

STAY CALM

"The LORD himself will fight for you. Just stay calm."

EXODUS 14:14 NLT

The Israelites were so happy when Moses led them out of Egypt! But when they got to the Red Sea, they started to panic. Pharaoh's army was chasing them, and now they were trapped! But Moses told them to calm down and trust God. God had promised to save them, and God always keeps His promises.

When everything is going your way, faith in God is easy. But when things get hard, don't panic! God is still with you. Keep praying, and find comfort in His promise to give you all you need. Remember His goodness. Strong faith can help you stay calm no matter what happens!

THOUGHT OF THE DAY

Keep your faith strong by reading Bible stories and talking to God!

PRAY TODAY

Dear God, please strengthen my faith so I can stay calm and trust You, no matter what happens. Amen.

CHOOSE GOD'S WAY

"Choose this day whom you will serve. . . . But as for me and my house, we will serve the Lord."

JOSHUA 24:15 ESV

D
o you know what it means to be free? When you are free, you are able to make choices. Since you're still young, your parents probably help you make good choices each day. But there are lots of decisions you can still make for yourself!

Your choices make a big difference in how your day will go. Will you choose to be kind or mean? Will you choose to share or be selfish? Will you choose to obey the rules or break the rules? When you have to make a choice, stop and think about what the Lord would have you do. Then choose His way. It is always good.

THOUGHT OF THE DAY

Lots of choices, big and small. Let God help you with them all!

PRAY TODAY

Dear God, thank You for giving me the freedom to make choices. Please help me to choose to do things Your way. Amen.

GOD FIRST

"Seek first God's kingdom and what God wants. Then all your other needs will be met as well."

MATTHEW 6:33 NCV

Have you ever wanted something new? It's fun to get new clothes and new toys. But God doesn't want us to forget all the things He's already given us. He tells us to put Him first. So here's an easy way to practice that. Before you ask for something new, thank God for all His great gifts! Do you have a happy family? A fun pet? A cozy jacket? Then ask God for ways to make Him happy, like sharing some of your things with others. It's OK to be excited about new things. But just remember—God comes first!

THOUGHT OF THE DAY

When God is first, you already have all you need!

PRAY TODAY

Dear God, thank You for all the ways You've blessed me. Help me remember to put You first every day! Amen.

HARD CHANGES

There is a time for everything, and a season for every activity under the heavens.

ECCLESIASTES 3:1 NIV

Some changes are easy. You can probably change your pajamas with no problem! But some changes—even good ones—can be hard. Moving to a new town or starting a different grade in school or welcoming a new sibling are all big changes that can bring lots of feelings. You might feel happy, sad, excited, mad, and nervous all at the same time. That's perfectly OK! Talk to your parents about it. Ask about a time they went through a big change. And remember to pray too. God can use changes to help you grow, learn, and find joy!

THOUGHT OF THE DAY

One thing NEVER changes: God's love!

PRAY TODAY

Dear God, sometimes I don't want things to change. Help me remember Your love and find joy in each new thing! Amen.

STRONG HEARTS

Those with pure hearts shall become stronger and stronger.

JOB 17:9B TLB

If you want to have strong muscles, you can practice running and do exercises. But how do you get a stronger heart? The Bible says that we can get strong hearts by practicing pure things.

Pure things are actions that help you follow God. You can learn Scripture verses, sing songs of praise, and watch and read stories that teach you how to be more like Jesus. When you spend your time doing things like that, your heart gets stronger. And with a strong heart, it's easier to do things God's way!

THOUGHT OF THE DAY

What's something you are doing to make your heart strong and pure?

PRAY TODAY

Dear God, please help me to follow You, so that my heart can grow strong and pure. Amen.

@ @ @ @ @ @ @

GOD GUIDES YOUR STEPS

A man's heart plans his way, but the Lord determines his steps.

PROVERBS 16:9 HCSB

What do you want to be when you grow up? It's so much fun to dream about the future! And now is the perfect time to learn all you can about the things you love to do.

God wants you to work hard for your dreams. But He also wants you to stay close to Him and listen to His direction. We can make plans, but the Bible says God directs our steps. So be sure to keep praying and listening to God. He will tell you which way to go so you end up where He knows you should be!

THOUGHT OF THE DAY

Your future is in good hands—God's!

PRAY TODAY

Dear God, I'm so excited to become who You want me to be! Help me listen to Your direction and work hard. Amen.

GOD'S ALWAYS THERE

"Do not be afraid or discouraged. For the LORD your God is with you wherever you go."

JOSHUA 1:9 NLT

When you have a great day, it's easy to remember God! You might even feel extra close to Him. But when you have a bad day, guess what? God is still right beside you.

We all go through hard times. And it's normal to feel lonely during those times. But you are never truly alone because God will never leave you. And you can talk with Him about anything! He loves to comfort you. So next time you feel upset or lonely, imagine God giving you a big hug. He's always around!

THOUGHT OF THE DAY

God's beside you every day. Nothing makes Him go away.

PRAY TODAY

Dear God, I'm so glad You will never leave me. Help me remember to talk to You when I'm feeling down. Amen.

DIFFERENT GIFTS

We have different gifts, according to the grace given to each of us.

ROMANS 12:6A NIV

One day, Jesus visited His friends Mary and Martha. Martha decided to cook Jesus a meal and clean the house for Him, while Mary sat and listened to Him talk. Martha felt upset because Mary wasn't helping her. But Jesus said that Mary's work was important too: she was listening and learning!

We all have different gifts we can use to serve God. Maybe you like to sing or tell people about Jesus. Maybe you make yummy cookies to share with friends or you love to pray for others. Don't worry about how other people show their love for God. Instead, work on practicing your own gifts!

THOUGHT OF THE DAY

What is something you're good at? How can you use that to serve God?

PRAY TODAY

Dear God, please stop me from comparing my gifts with others'. Show me how I can serve You well! Amen.

GENTLE AND CALM

Always be gentle with others. The Lord will soon be here.

PHILIPPIANS 4:5 CEV

God says to be gentle with each other. What does that mean?

We're gentle when we act calmly. It can be hard to control our bodies and words sometimes. But when you speak or behave roughly, you might hurt someone! You could hurt their bodies by hitting or pushing. You could hurt their feelings by yelling. Remember that everyone is part of God's family—even people who make you mad. And God doesn't want any of His children to get hurt. So ask Him to help you choose gentleness all the time!

THOUGHT OF THE DAY

When you feel out of control, try taking a deep breath before you do anything. It will give you time to choose a gentle action!

PRAY TODAY

Dear God, sometimes it's SO HARD to be gentle. Help me calm down so I can treat everyone gently every day. Amen.

PARTY TIME!

So rejoice in the L<small>ORD</small> and be glad, all you who obey him! Shout for joy, all you whose hearts are pure!

PSALM 32:11 NLT

Can you think of a time you went to a party? Maybe you had a birthday party, or you celebrated a big holiday with your family. Isn't it fun to be happy and joyful together?

Guess what? You could have a party every day just by praising God! He is so good, and He loves us very much. He gave us the Bible so we could get to know Him and learn how to live a great life. He even sent Jesus so we can live with Him forever. Those are all reasons to celebrate! So sing, dance, and tell your friends. It's a God party!

THOUGHT OF THE DAY

If you threw a God party, what would it look like?

PRAY TODAY

Dear God, hooray for You! I am so glad to be Your child, and I want to celebrate You every day! Amen.

THE RIGHT TIME

There is a right time for everything. . . . A time to cry; a time to laugh; a time to grieve; a time to dance.

ECCLESIASTES 3:1, 4 TLB

No one feels the same way all the time. God knows that, and He tells us in the Bible that it's OK to have times when we feel sad and other times when we feel like laughing. Times when we get angry and other times when we feel like giving someone a hug. Feelings change, but one thing that never changes is God's love for us. It is always the right time for that!

THOUGHT OF THE DAY

God is good all the time! All the time God is good!

PRAY TODAY

Dear God, thank You for giving me so many feelings and for loving me all the time. Amen.

LOVE AND HONOR

Love each other with genuine affection, and take delight in honoring each other.

ROMANS 12:10 NLT

One of the best ways to make good friends is to be a good friend! But do you know how to do that?

God gives us some clues! First, love your friends. When you love people, you treat them kindly and help when they're having a hard time. Then, He asks us to honor our friends. Have you ever cheered for a friend who's playing a soccer game or performing in the talent show? Those are both great ways to honor your friends. And when you love and honor others, chances are they will love and honor you too!

THOUGHT OF THE DAY

Honoring friends should be fun! What's a creative way to celebrate someone today?

PRAY TODAY

Dear God, thank You for good friends! Please show me ways to love and honor others every day! Amen.

WIN OR LOSE

Happiness comes to those who are fair to others and are always just and good.

PSALM 106:3 TLB

D o you like playing games? Who do you like to play with? It's most fun to play a game with people who follow the rules, right?

Following the rules of a game means you won't always win. And that's OK! Losing can be disappointing, but you can still have fun playing. The most important thing is to play fair. Don't try to break the rules just so you can win. That's called cheating, and it's no fun for anyone else. Instead, try your best, and say "Hooray!" for whoever wins! Everyone loves to play with someone who plays fair and has fun.

THOUGHT OF THE DAY

What's your favorite game?

PRAY TODAY

Dear God, sometimes it's so hard to lose. Please help me feel peaceful and calm, no matter who wins. Amen.

TIME WITH GOD

"But when you pray, go into your private room, shut your door, and pray to your Father who is in secret."

MATTHEW 6:6A HCSB

What does your usual day look like? Maybe you have a special way you get ready for school in the morning. Maybe you have story time before bed. To make your day the best it can be, set aside some time with God too!

Jesus said the best way to spend time with God is to pray. Talk to Him just like you would talk to a best friend! Ask Him your questions and tell Him your ideas. Talk about what's worrying you. Share a funny story! God loves to hear from you. So find a special place and spend some time with Him each day.

THOUGHT OF THE DAY

To have the best talks with God, find a place without a lot of distractions!

PRAY TODAY

Dear God, I want to be better friends with You. Please help me make time every day so we can talk together! Amen.

GOD KEEPS HIS PROMISES

Those who know Your name will put their trust in You. For You, O Lord, have never left alone those who look for You.

PSALM 9:10 NLV

Sometimes it's easy to see God working in your life. But other times, it's hard to know what He's up to. Maybe you didn't get on a team you'd hoped to join, or a good friend moved away and you feel lonely. Maybe you prayed for something, and it didn't happen. Don't worry—God still hears you! Remember God's good promises: He loves you, He listens to you, He'll never leave you, and He has good plans for you. God never breaks a promise. So keep on praying, and keep on trusting. He is always by your side.

THOUGHT OF THE DAY

Jesus loves you, this you know. He will never let you go.

PRAY TODAY

Dear God, I trust that You're with me. When I'm having a hard day, please remind me of all Your good promises. Amen.

YOU CAN DO ANYTHING!

Jesus replied, "Why do you say 'if you can'? Anything is possible for someone who has faith!"

MARK 9:23 CEV

What is something big you want to do? It's exciting to have dreams and goals! God tells us to dream big, work hard, and have faith in Him. He has great plans for you, and He can help you accomplish anything.

Sometimes that's hard to remember. Maybe learning a new skill takes longer than you thought it would, or somebody says something discouraging. Don't give up! Go back to God and remember His promises. Have faith that He loves you and cares about your dreams. Trust that He will never leave you. With God by your side, nothing is impossible!

THOUGHT OF THE DAY

Your big dreams are gifts from God. He gave them to you for a reason!

PRAY TODAY

Dear God, thank You for caring about the things I care about. Help me have strong faith in You as I dream big dreams! Amen.

POWERFUL KINDNESS

"Do what is right and true. Be kind and merciful to each other."

ZECHARIAH 7:9B NCV

Zechariah was a man who told people about God. One day, the people asked Zechariah what God wanted them to do. Do you know the only thing God asked for? Kindness.

That's because kindness is super powerful! Think about everything kindness can do. It can encourage a frustrated friend. It can comfort a sad neighbor. When you choose kind words, you can stop someone's anger or heal someone's embarrassment. With kindness and patience, you can even teach others new things. If anyone wants you to act in unkind ways, don't fall for it! God knows that caring for others is the most powerful choice of all!

THOUGHT OF THE DAY

Kindness comes in lots of forms: patience and generosity are good places to start!

PRAY TODAY

Dear God, I want to be powerful! Please help me choose kindness every day. Amen.

INSIDE OR OUTSIDE

"God does not see the same way people see. People look at the outside of a person, but the LORD looks at the heart."

1 SAMUEL 16:7B NCV

David was the youngest and smallest kid in his family. But God still chose him to be king! That's because David loved God with his whole heart.

Do you ever worry about what you look like? Guess what? God doesn't! He looks right past the outside to what's inside you! He sees your heart, and that's all that matters to Him. And that's how He wants us to see others too. So don't worry about the way you look or the clothes you wear. When your heart loves God and cares for others, you're beautiful!

THOUGHT OF THE DAY

Try to see others the way God sees you—heart first!

PRAY TODAY

Dear God, thank You for loving me just the way I am. Please give me a heart that makes You happy! Amen.

GOOD FRUIT

But the fruit of the Spirit is love, joy, peace, patience, kindness, goodness, faithfulness, gentleness, self-control; against such things there is no law.

GALATIANS 5:22–23 ESV

Do you know how fruit grows in a garden? Every delicious strawberry or bright tomato comes from a tiny seed, planted in good soil and watered often. The Bible says you are like a seed in a garden, and God is the rich soil and fresh water you need. When you follow Him, you will grow strong and produce wonderful things.

Maybe joy and peace will sprout at unexpected times! Or gentleness will bloom, even when you feel angry. Or self-control will ripen right when you need it! So spend time with God by praying and reading the Bible. Think of it as watering your garden!

THOUGHT OF THE DAY

Reread today's verse. What fruit do you want to grow in your heart?

PRAY TODAY

Dear God, please help me follow You closely so that I can grow good fruit! Amen.

SHARE A SMILE

Happiness makes a person smile, but sadness can break a person's spirit.

PROVERBS 15:13 NCV

How do you feel when you see someone smiling? Does it make you feel happy too? Maybe you want to check out what's making them cheerful! Maybe you feel warm inside because that smile means they're happy to see you. When you're feeling sad, just seeing someone smile can help you feel better.

You can share your smile too. Try it out! When you see a friend or someone you know, try smiling at them first and see how many friends you can get to smile back. Pretty soon, you'll be an expert at spreading happiness.

THOUGHT OF THE DAY
Smiles are the easiest things to share. There are always enough to go around!

PRAY TODAY
Dear God, I'm glad I can share happiness with others. Thank You for the gift of smiles!
Amen.

HOW GOD LOVES

This is what real love is: It is not our love for God; it is God's love for us. He sent his Son to die in our place to take away our sins.

1 JOHN 4:10 NCV

God's love is not just an idea. It is something He does for us. God knows that we don't always do what's right. He knows we need to be forgiven. So God sent Jesus to live a perfect life. Then Jesus died on the cross to pay the price for the wrong things we do, so we can be forgiven and live with Him forever.

God loved you before you were born. He cares about you now and will always love you. When you love and forgive others, you show God how much you love Him back.

THOUGHT OF THE DAY

God loves you and now you know it! Share His love by how you show it!

PRAY TODAY

Dear God, thank You for sending Jesus so I can be forgiven and know Your love. Please help me share Your love with others. Amen.

WHAT'S IT FOR?

Every part of Scripture is God-breathed and useful one way or another.

2 TIMOTHY 3:16A MSG

The Bible is full of great stories. Some are exciting and some are peaceful. Some are short and some are long—some are even told in poems! And God has something to teach us in each one.

The story of Joseph and his brothers in Genesis teaches us to be faithful and trust God. The story of Jesus meeting a woman at the well helps us understand God's love for all people. When you hear Bible stories, try to figure out what God wants you to learn. Every verse is there for a reason!

THOUGHT OF THE DAY

Who's your favorite Bible character? What's God teaching you through him or her?

PRAY TODAY

Dear God, I love to hear Bible stories. Help me listen closely so I can learn the things You want me to! Amen.

HOW TO KNOW GOD

This is how we are sure that we have come to know Him: by keeping His commands.

1 JOHN 2:3 HCSB

How can you really know God? Can you visit Him? Can you take him to Show and Tell? Can you invite Him to dinner? Not exactly! But the Bible says that we can know God by *doing* what He says.

We learn what God says by reading the Bible and going to church. Then we have to ACT! When we love one another, we love like God loves. When we tell the truth, we are doing what God does. We get closer to God when we act the way He tells us to. So if you want to know God, try following His commands!

THOUGHT OF THE DAY

Read your Bible and do what God says. That's the best way to know God better!

PRAY TODAY

Dear God, I want to know You better each day. Please help me do just what You say. Amen.

HAVING FUN

"He will yet fill your mouth with laughter and your lips with shouts of joy."

JOB 8:21 NIV

What makes you laugh? A tickle on your toes? A funny joke? A silly picture? God loves to see His children laugh. It makes Him happy to know that you are happy! Today, see if you can find something to laugh about. Maybe you will see a friend making a silly face or hear a funny story or sing a song with silly words. Maybe you'll make others laugh too! Laughing and having fun are both ways to show that we're filled with joy. When we are happy, that makes God happy too!

THOUGHT OF THE DAY

What kinds of things make you laugh?

PRAY TODAY

Dear God, thank You for loving me and for wanting me to be filled with joy! Amen.

WAITING PATIENTLY

I waited patiently for the LORD. He turned to me and heard my cry.

PSALM 40:1 NCV

God has good plans for you. He knows your dreams, and He wants to give you good things. He also knows the perfect time to give you everything you need. But it can be hard to wait for God's timing!

The Bible says to wait patiently for God. Patience means you trust God to do what He's promised. It means waiting with hope and excitement about what He has in store for you. Talk to God often. Ask Him to show you the best way to live each day. Share your ideas with Him. Then watch and see what He does! He won't let you down.

THOUGHT OF THE DAY

God hears every prayer. He's working on big plans for you!

PRAY TODAY

Dear God, thank You for hearing my prayers! Help me to trust You and wait patiently, even when it's hard. Amen.

YOU CAN ALWAYS TRUST GOD

Commit everything you do to the LORD. Trust him, and he will help you.

PSALM 37:5 NLT

You might not always understand what God is doing. But you can always trust that He is in control.

It's normal to want to be in charge of everything. Especially if you think your ideas are the best! But God wants us to remember that He's really in charge. So don't worry if things don't happen the way you expected. Try not to get upset if you don't get what you want right away. Pray for God's help, and trust Him to take care of you. He always will.

THOUGHT OF THE DAY

How does it feel to know that God is in control of everything?

PRAY TODAY

Dear God, help me remember that You control everything, not me! Thank You that I can trust You all the time. Amen.

PEACE ON THE INSIDE

Only God gives inward peace, and I depend on him.

PSALM 62:5 CEV

Have you ever wished you could change what's happening around you? Sometimes, things happen that we can't control. But God has a great gift for you: inward peace. Inward peace is when God helps you feel calm inside no matter what.

When you have peace on the inside, you can handle anything. If you're scared of the dark, God can help you feel less afraid. If school gets frustrating, God can help you slow down and find a solution. So don't worry if you have tough days or sad times. God's inward peace will help you through it all!

THOUGHT OF THE DAY

When you can't change what's outside, God can change what's inside!

PRAY TODAY

Dear God, I'm so glad You give me peace on the inside. It's one more way I know You're always with me. Amen.

WORK CHEERFULLY

Work hard and cheerfully at all you do.

COLOSSIANS 3:23A TLB

When you think of chores, do you feel cheerful? That might seem like a silly question! But God tells us to work hard AND to work cheerfully. So can you find ways to enjoy the work you have to do?

Maybe you can make up a game for getting all your chores finished. Or try making up a funny song like Larry does to help you study for school! Clean up your toys with a friend and race to see who can finish first. Surprise your mom and dad by doing stuff without being asked! When you have fun with your work, you'll do an even better job!

THOUGHT OF THE DAY

God loves a happy worker.

PRAY TODAY

Dear God, please show me how I can work cheerfully and do all my work well! Amen.

A PEACEFUL HOME

How wonderful, how beautiful, when brothers and sisters get along!

PSALM 133:1 MSG

It's not always easy to get along with everyone in a family! Maybe your brother or sister doesn't like playing the game you like, or a cousin broke a favorite toy. Maybe you don't want to do your chores. The problem is, arguing just makes everyone frustrated. Instead, ask God to help you find solutions.

Can you take turns choosing games with your siblings? Or put away special toys when cousins come over? Can you figure out how to finish all your chores quickly? It's OK to feel upset sometimes. Just ask God to help you make things peaceful again. Your family will thank you!

THOUGHT OF THE DAY

What can you do to make your home more peaceful?

PRAY TODAY

Dear God, sometimes I get upset with my family. Please help me find ways to make my home a peaceful one! Amen.

GOD BLESSED YOU

Every good gift and every perfect gift is from above, coming down from the Father of lights.

JAMES 1:17 ESV

Are you interested in something unique? Maybe you feel out of place, because no one seems to be just like you. Or maybe you feel like there's nothing very special about you at all! Here's the truth: God has blessed you with good gifts He chose just for you. And He wants you to use them! Your gifts could be talents, like singing or playing sports. Your gifts could be attributes, like being kind, generous, or wise. Maybe you're a great leader or an excellent listener. Ask God to show you the gifts He's given you. Then practice using them every day!

THOUGHT OF THE DAY

Every gift God gives is good. Are you using yours? You should!

PRAY TODAY

Dear God, please help me see my gifts, and show me how to use them! Amen.

WHAT TIME IS IT?

There is a time for everything. . . . a time to be silent and a time to speak.

ECCLESIASTES 3:1, 7 NIV

The Bible says sometimes it is important to be silent and listen, and other times it is important to talk. Some listening times are when you are at school or at church and another person is telling you a story. Some talking times are when it is your turn to share about something you know or when you have something important to tell a friend or your mom and dad. We learn about things by talking *and* by listening. It's important to know what time it is!

THOUGHT OF THE DAY

If you want others to listen to you, you should also be a good listener!

PRAY TODAY

Dear God, thank You for always listening to me. Help me know when I should talk and when I should listen. Amen.

HIS PROMISES ARE GUARANTEED

"Do not be afraid or discouraged. For the LORD your God is with you wherever you go."

JOSHUA 1:9 NLT

The stories in the Bible tell us something wonderful: God keeps His promises! What are God's promises? God loves you. He gives strength to people when they feel weak or afraid. He always hears your prayers. He will give you everything you need. Nothing will ever separate you from God's love. And because of Jesus, we can live with Him forever in heaven. Those are some pretty big promises!

Sometimes people make big promises they can't keep. But you never have to worry about that with God. His promises are guaranteed!

THOUGHT OF THE DAY

God's promises are always true; He's watching out for me and you!

PRAY TODAY

Dear God, thank You for always keeping Your promises! I know that I can trust You. Amen.

GOD COMES FIRST

"Do not have other gods besides Me."

EXODUS 20:3 HCSB

God gave us a list of good rules called the Ten Commandments. Some rules tell us how to live with others, but the first three are all about how we should live with God. That's because God should always come first in our life. We should love Him with our whole heart, and nothing should ever become more important than God. And when we use God's name, we should always talk about Him with love and respect. Those rules are listed before the others because when we love God first, loving others is easy!

THOUGHT OF THE DAY

Put God first each day—say a prayer as soon as you wake up!

PRAY TODAY

Dear God, sometimes I forget that You are most important. Help me put You first and love You well. Amen.

LIVE IN PEACE

It is good and pleasant when God's people live together in peace!

PSALM 133:1 NCV

Every day you get to decide how you'll act with the people you meet. So why not decide to get along? When you get along with others, that's called living peacefully.

If a friend wants to play something different, give it a try! When you meet someone new, say hello with a smile. If someone says something mean, choose to respond with kind words instead of angry ones. You might meet people who like to argue instead of being peaceful. Don't worry! You still get to control how YOU act. And who knows? You might just convince them to give peace a chance too!

THOUGHT OF THE DAY

What's one way you can brighten someone's day today?

PRAY TODAY

Dear God, please help me get along with the people around me. I want to live peacefully with everyone! Amen.

LOST AND FOUND

"What man among you, who has 100 sheep and loses one of them, does not leave the 99 in the open field and go after the lost one until he finds it?"

LUKE 15:4 HCSB

Have you ever lost something precious? Maybe you searched and searched for it, forgetting about anything else until you found it. Finding something you've lost feels so wonderful!

Jesus says that's how He feels about you. You are incredibly precious to Him. When you feel lost or alone, He will search for you. He will find ways to reach out and remind you of His love, and He won't stop until you're safely back in His arms. And when you're back, He'll celebrate! Because you are God's treasure, and He loves you.

THOUGHT OF THE DAY

No matter how lost you feel, you are never far from God.

PRAY TODAY

Dear God, when I feel sad or lonely or make bad choices, thank You for always bringing me back home! Amen.

COURAGE TO WAIT

Wait for the LORD; be strong, and let your heart take courage; wait for the LORD!

PSALM 27:14 ESV

When you think of courage you might think of doing something really exciting! But sometimes the bravest thing you can do is trust God and wait for Him to work.

God promised the great Bible hero Joshua that he would capture the town of Jericho. But Joshua had to spend seven days just walking around the town. It must have been hard to wait! But Joshua trusted that God would fulfill His promise, and on the seventh day, He did! Next time you're having a hard time waiting for something to happen, remember Joshua. Trust God to do big things at just the right time!

THOUGHT OF THE DAY

What's something you're waiting for?

PRAY TODAY

Dear God, it's hard to wait! Please give me courage to trust You. Amen.

GOD GIVES WISDOM

If any of you lacks wisdom, you should ask God, who gives generously to all without finding fault, and it will be given to you.

JAMES 1:5 NIV

Sometimes the Veggies get stuck. Maybe Larry and Bob are arguing. Or Junior doesn't know how to make a new friend. Or Petunia can't solve a tricky problem.

Do you ever feel that way? It takes wisdom to figure out hard things! Fortunately, God is always wise. And the Bible promises that if you ask God, He will give wisdom to you! You don't have to be smart enough to solve all your problems. You just need to be smart enough to ask God to help you!

THOUGHT OF THE DAY

God's wisdom is always good and true. Just ask! He'll give it freely to you.

PRAY TODAY

Dear God, I am so glad You promise to give me wisdom. Please help me remember to ask You when I don't know what to do. Amen.

LOVE YOUR NEIGHBOR

If you really keep the royal law according to the Scripture, "Love your neighbor as yourself," you are doing right.

JAMES 2:8 NIV

The Bible says that if you love your neighbor, you're doing a great job. But does that mean you should just love the people in your neighborhood? Nope! According to God, a neighbor can be anyone! Is a classmate feeling lonely? Sit next to him at lunch. Is your sister frustrated learning something new? Help or encourage her! Even people in other parts of the world are your neighbors! You can help them by praying for them or supporting missionaries who bring God's Word to faraway places. Loving your neighbor is important work!

THOUGHT OF THE DAY

Who is a "neighbor" you can love today?

PRAY TODAY

Dear God, thank You for all my neighbors! Help me love each one I meet today. Amen.

A POWERFUL LIFE

For the kingdom of God is not a matter of talk but of power.

1 CORINTHIANS 4:20 NIV

God wants you to live an "empowered life." That means you don't just sit around and talk about things you wish would happen. It means you *make* things happen!

Choosing to follow God is the first step to an empowered life. God can give you courage to try new things and make new friends. He can give you joy, even when bad things happen. He can show you how to help people around you in new, creative ways.

So what do you want to do? Ask God for the power to do it!

THOUGHT OF THE DAY

God's power has no limits—so neither should your ideas!

PRAY TODAY

Dear God, thank You for sharing Your power with me! Help me make exciting things happen in Your name! Amen.

YOU AND GOD CAN DO IT!

As Goliath moved closer to attack, David quickly ran out to meet him.

1 SAMUEL 17:48 NLT

In the story of David and Goliath, David isn't the kind of hero you'd expect. He's not a trained soldier. In fact, he's only at the battlefield to bring food to his brothers. But when no one else will fight the scary giant Goliath, David volunteers. He trusts that God will help him, and runs right out to face Goliath. And he wins!

Is there something you need to do that's making you nervous? God can help! He made you to do exciting, brave, and important things. So pray and ask for His help. When you trust in Him, you can do anything!

THOUGHT OF THE DAY

When you feel nervous, just recall, that God can help you do it all!

PRAY TODAY

Dear God, thank You for helping me do great things! Help me trust You whenever I feel afraid. Amen.

GOD, THE GREAT TEACHER

If you don't know what you're doing, pray to the Father. He loves to help.

JAMES 1:5 MSG

If you want to get better at something, it helps to have a great teacher. God wants you to grow in wisdom—and He's the best teacher there is!

What does it mean to grow in wisdom? It means you're always looking for ways to make God happy. It means you make friends with people who are different from you, because God loves everyone. It means you find ways to be kind and caring. And if you don't know what to do, it means your first step is talking to God. He'll teach you everything you need to know!

THOUGHT OF THE DAY

Are you not sure which way to go? Pray, and God will let you know!

PRAY TODAY

Dear God, thank You for being the best teacher! Please help me grow in wisdom every day. Amen.

@ @ @ @ @ @ @ @

LIGHTEN YOUR LOAD

Worry is a heavy burden, but a kind word always brings cheer.

PROVERBS 12:25 CEV

God wants us to be happy in His world. He's given us good friends and families, and special talents. But we can't enjoy all He's done if we're stuck with a bunch of worries.

When you're worried all the time, it's like dragging around a giant suitcase. You get tired and grouchy, and you can't go very far! God wants to take all your worries away so you can live the life He's planned for you. So next time you start worrying, imagine handing your suitcase to God. Then find something you can thank Him for!

THOUGHT OF THE DAY

The Bible says a kind word can bring cheer. Try sharing kind words with yourself!

PRAY TODAY

Dear God, I don't like carrying around heavy worries. Please take my worries away so I can enjoy You more. Amen.

BUILD SELF-CONTROL

To your knowledge, add self-control; and to your self-control, add patience.

2 PETER 1:6 NCV

When you want something, you probably want it right away. But that's not usually how things work! That's where patience and self-control come in.

God wants us to learn self-control because He knows good things take time. And hurrying causes mistakes! If you don't practice, you won't learn to play an instrument or perform a dance well. If you push someone out of line so you can go first, you'll probably get in trouble. So ask God to help you build self-control. He will give you strength and patience so you can grow and learn all you need to!

THOUGHT OF THE DAY

Next time you want to rush through something, stop and ask God to help you go slow!

PRAY TODAY

Dear God, please help me build self-control so I can learn new things and be a good friend! Amen.

PRACTICE LOVING

Dear friends, let us practice loving each other, for love comes from God and those who are loving and kind show that they are the children of God, and that they are getting to know him better.

1 JOHN 4:7 TLB

'll bet you already know that practice is important if you want to get better at playing a game, reading, or making music. But the Bible says we also need to practice loving each other! We can do that by thinking of ways to be kind. Sharing, taking turns, offering to help, giving a hug, and saying "please" and "thanks" are all ways to be kind. You could surprise your mom by doing chores or give toys to kids who don't have much. Look around at home and at school. Who needs some extra love today? Can you think of ways to practice loving them?

THOUGHT OF THE DAY

If you want to live God's way, practice loving every day!

PRAY TODAY

Dear God, I want to love like You love. Please help me find ways to practice loving today. Amen.

GOD CAN HELP

Depend on the Lord and his strength. Always go to him for help.

1 CHRONICLES 16:11 ICB

Do you ever feel like you don't know what to do? Do you sometimes need an idea about how to solve a problem? The Bible says that you can depend on the Lord and His strength. That means He won't let you down. You can ask God to help you when you need answers to your problems. He loves to hear from you, and He wants to give you courage, strength, and wisdom. Even if it's a big, big problem, nothing is too hard for God. You are His precious child, and He promises to be your helper.

THOUGHT OF THE DAY

God is there to help you through whatever seems too hard to do!

PRAY TODAY

Dear God, thank You for loving me and for always being there to help me. Amen.

CHOOSE COURAGE

"This is my command—be strong and courageous! Do not be afraid or discouraged. For the LORD your God is with you wherever you go."

JOSHUA 1:9 NLT

You make choices every day. What toy will you play with? What colors will you use in your painting? How many cherries will you put on your ice cream sundae?

Some choices are small, but others are pretty big! How will you treat people? Will you tell the truth? God wants you to make good choices about big things. That's why He gives us a helpful first step: always choose courage! It takes courage to be kind when others are not, or to tell the truth when we're afraid we might get in trouble.

THOUGHT OF THE DAY

When you choose courage first, it's easier to decide what comes next!

PRAY TODAY

Dear God, please help me see the choices I should make. Then give me the courage to make them! Amen.

MAKE TODAY HAPPY

What joy for those who can live in your house, always singing your praises. What joy for those whose strength comes from the LORD.

PSALM 84:4-5 NLT

Each day is a new gift from God. That's a pretty happy thought, isn't it?

But some days, you might not feel very happy. That's OK. God can still help you find joy—which is even stronger than happiness! God is good, and He loves you. That never changes. Try praising God for the great things He's done. Find something—anything!—to thank Him for.

It's easy to praise God when you're feeling great. But looking for joy when you don't feel like it makes you strong in the Lord. And that's a happy thought!

THOUGHT OF THE DAY

When you go looking for joy, you'll always find it!

PRAY TODAY

Dear God, thank You that Your love never changes. Help me find reasons to be happy every day! Amen.

LIVING TOGETHER

How good and how pleasant it is when God's people live together in unity!

PSALM 133:1 NIV

Who lives with you at your house? Some families are large, and some are small; but God says that it is always good when we live together in unity. Unity means that even though we are different from each other, we try to get along. Sometimes you will get your way, but sometimes someone else gets their way. Sometimes you get to do your favorite thing or have your favorite food for dinner. Sometimes it is someone else's turn to have their favorites. It isn't always easy to get along, but it makes God happy when we try.

THOUGHT OF THE DAY

What are some ways your family has fun together?

PRAY TODAY

Dear God, thank You for giving me my family. Please help me to do my part to live in unity with everyone here. Amen.

ASK YOUR PARENTS

The one who lives with integrity is righteous; his children who come after him will be happy.

PROVERBS 20:7 HCSB

Your parents work hard to help you learn and grow. One of the best ways parents can help is by sharing all the cool stuff they know.

You can talk to your parents about anything! Are you working on a problem at school? Do you want to know more about God? Maybe you just have a hard time following the rules. Your parents can help you think through troubles and learn new things too. Maybe they've even had some of the same troubles you're facing! Your parents love you and want you to be happy. They are a wonderful gift from God!

THOUGHT OF THE DAY

Ask your mom or dad what they've learned from their parents!

PRAY TODAY

Dear God, thank You for my loving parents! I'm so glad I can learn so much from them. Amen.

A LISTENING EAR

"Then you will call upon Me and go and pray to Me, and I will listen to you."

JEREMIAH 29:12 NKJV

Sometimes it can feel like no one hears what you say. But God is always listening! The Bible says that whenever you talk to God, He will listen to you. He listens because He loves you so much! It doesn't matter what you talk about. You can tell Him what makes you happy or sad. You can tell Him what happened during the day or talk through a problem you're trying to solve. You can even sing Him a song! Whatever you have to say, however you want to say it, God loves to hear your voice.

THOUGHT OF THE DAY

God listens to every word. Always know that you've been heard!

PRAY TODAY

Dear God, I'm so glad You listen to my prayers. Thank You for always loving me and caring for me. Amen.

GIVING AND RECEIVING

"Give, and you will receive. Your gift will return to you in full—pressed down, shaken together, running over, and poured into your lap. The amount you give will determine the amount you get back."

LUKE 6:38 NLT

Boys and girls who share always seem to have lots of friends. Others want to play with them, and they end up having more and more fun. The Bible says that's because when we give, then we will receive. When we give away kindness and share with others, we receive kindness from others, and they want to share with us! Giving and receiving work together to bring God's blessings to everyone!

THOUGHT OF THE DAY

What will you choose to give to someone else today?

PRAY TODAY

Dear God, thank You for giving so much to me. Help me to be a good giver today. Amen.

BELIEVE WHAT GOD SAYS!

Abraham trusted God, and when God told him to leave home and go far away to another land that he promised to give him, Abraham obeyed. Away he went, not even knowing where he was going.

HEBREWS 11:8 TLB

God told Abraham to go to a special land He'd prepared for Abraham and his family. But God didn't say how to get there! Still, Abraham and his wife trusted God. They knew His promises are always good, so they gathered their things and started walking. And God led them exactly where they were supposed to go!

When you do what God asks, you show that you trust Him too. Maybe He wants you to be patient with your siblings or tell someone you're sorry. It isn't always easy to do what God asks, but it's always a good idea!

THOUGHT OF THE DAY

What is something you think God wants you to do?

PRAY TODAY

Dear God, I want to trust You like Abraham did. Please help me do the things You ask me to! Amen.

THE WAY, THE TRUTH, AND THE LIFE

Jesus answered, "I am the way and the truth and the life. No one comes to the Father except through me."

JOHN 14:6 NIV

One day, Jesus told His disciples that He is three things: the way, the truth, and the life. He is the way because He shows us the way to live. When we follow His example, we treat others kindly and make good choices. He is the truth because everything He says is true. We can always trust what Jesus says! And He is the life because when we believe in Him we can live with God in heaven forever.

Jesus is everything you need. So trust Him with everything you have!

THOUGHT OF THE DAY

Jesus always says what's true and offers all good things to you!

PRAY TODAY

Dear God, thank You for sending Jesus to show me the way, to tell me the truth about You, and to invite me to live with You forever. I love You! Amen.

BE A FAITHFUL FOLLOWER

I have chosen the way of faithfulness; I set your rules before me.

PSALM 119:30 ESV

Being faithful to God means choosing to follow God's rules, even if it's hard. We can show God we love Him by practicing faithfulness.

Being faithful doesn't just make God happy—it can make you happy too! God's rules are designed to give you the very best life. God tells us to be honest because He knows that's how to have great friendships. He tells us not to say mean things, because He knows that would make us and others sad. He tells us to be generous with what we have because sharing shows love. Choosing faithfulness to God means choosing happiness!

THOUGHT OF THE DAY

God's rules are like a secret code to living a great life!

PRAY TODAY

Dear God, it's not always easy to follow rules. But I know Your rules are good! Please help me choose Your way. Amen.

DO WHAT'S RIGHT

Don't get tired of helping others. You will be rewarded when the time is right if you don't give up.

GALATIANS 6:9 CEV

Making right choices is always good, but sometimes it is hard to do. Maybe your friends are making a poor choice and they want you to do the same thing. What will you do then?

It helps to remember that God loves you and is watching over you. He wants to help you do what is right, even when it's hard. Ask Him to give you courage to make good choices. He promises to surprise you with blessings when you follow Him!

THOUGHT OF THE DAY

When you need to make a choice about doing what is right, always ask God for His help.

PRAY TODAY

Dear God, I'm so glad You love me and want me to do what is right. Help me remember to call on You when I have to make hard choices. Amen.

@ @ @ @ @ @ @

THE WISDOM OF TRUTH

You want me to be completely truthful, so teach me wisdom.

PSALM 51:6 NCV

D o you ever feel like lying is easier than telling the truth? Sometimes it seems that way. But God says the truth is always the wise choice.

When you tell a lie, you might get what you want right away. But you'll probably have to make up more lies to keep the truth a secret! You might feel sad or scared inside. You might even end up hurting someone else. But with the truth, there's none of those bad feelings! So instead, ask God to give you the wisdom and courage to tell the truth. The truth pleases God, and it's best for everyone!

THOUGHT OF THE DAY

When others know you say what's true, they'll want to be good friends with you!

PRAY TODAY

Dear God, sometimes I'm tempted to lie. Help me to be wise and brave every day, so I will always choose the truth. Amen.

WHAT DO YOU HAVE?

Don't set your heart on anything that is your neighbor's.

EXODUS 20:17B MSG

Do you and your friends have exactly the same toys? Of course not! Sharing new things makes playing together really fun. But sometimes, you might feel upset when a friend gets something you want. When you let that bad feeling become bigger than the good feelings of playing together, that's called *jealousy*. And it's no fun for anyone! God doesn't want you to feel that way. That's why He says to remember the good things you already have! Everyone has good gifts from God. What are yours? When you're happy with what you have, you can be happy for others too!

THOUGHT OF THE DAY

If your friend gets something really cool, celebrate! Then you'll *both* be happy!

PRAY TODAY

Dear God, please help me remember the good things I have. I don't want to be jealous—I want to be happy! Amen.

LOVE YOUR WHOLE FAMILY

But Ruth said, "Don't beg me to leave you or to stop following you. Where you go, I will go. Where you live, I will live. Your people will be my people, and your God will be my God."

RUTH 1:16 NCV

The most important thing in any family is love. You should always show love to each person in your family. And you should always, always feel loved!

Ruth knew how to love her family well. When her husband died, she stayed with her mother-in-law, Naomi, and worked hard to take care of her. Naomi loved Ruth as well, and she cared for her by sharing wisdom and good advice. With Naomi's help, Ruth got married again, and one of her descendants was Jesus!

Everyone in a family has a role to play. When you all look out for one another, great things can happen!

THOUGHT OF THE DAY

How does your family show love to each other?

PRAY TODAY

Dear Lord, please help me remember that loving You and my family are more important than anything! Amen.

BUT FIRST, GOD!

This is the day the LORD has made; let us rejoice and be glad in it.

PSALM 118:24 ESV

What do you do when you wake up each morning? Do you brush your teeth? Wash your face? You probably eat breakfast, and I hope you get dressed! There's a lot to do once you're out of bed. But here's something you can do while you're still snuggled in your blankets: pray! Each new day is a gift from God. Thank Him for today and for all the wonderful plans He has in store for you. Ask for His help with anything you're worried about. Praise Him for His love and goodness. It's always a good idea to start your day with God!

THOUGHT OF THE DAY
Wake up and pray, "Hooray for today!"

PRAY TODAY
Dear God, thank You for each and every day You give me! I love the world You have made. Amen.

THE JOY OF THE LORD

"For the joy of the Lord is your strength. You must not be dejected and sad!"

NEHEMIAH 8:10B TLB

Everyone feels sad sometimes. And that's OK! But God says we don't need to stay sad. No matter what happens around us, we can always find joy in the Lord. And that joy is strong enough to pull us out of sadness.

The joy of the Lord isn't the same as feeling happy about winning a game or eating a cupcake. It's knowing that God loves you, He's in control, and He'll never leave. So try looking for God's joy all day every day. The more often you find it, the stronger you'll be. Then you can face anything!

THOUGHT OF THE DAY

When you find God's joy, you'll know it. You'll feel strong and peaceful!

PRAY TODAY

Dear God, thank You for the gift of Your joy! Please help me find it any time I'm feeling sad. Amen.

@ @ @ @ @ @ @ @

BE KIND TO EVERYBODY

Be kind to one another, tenderhearted, forgiving one another, as God in Christ forgave you.

EPHESIANS 4:32 ESV

God is very clear: He wants you to treat everyone with kindness. But what if someone isn't kind to you? The rules don't change! That's because God loves each of us equally, no matter how we act.

The good news is, God can help you choose kindness. If someone says or does something unkind, try to stay calm. You can always decide to walk away or say something nice instead. Ask God to help you be patient and forgive quickly. He will bless you when you try to be kind!

THOUGHT OF THE DAY

Sometimes people are not kind because no one has shown them how to be. Show someone kindness today!

PRAY TODAY

Dear God, please help me to be kind and patient with everyone, even when it's hard. Amen.

@ @ @ @ @ @ @ @

GOD'S FAVORITE GIFT

"Praise the name of God forever and ever, for he has all wisdom and power."

DANIEL 2:20 NLT

What's the best gift you've ever received? Did you know that God loves to receive gifts too? But He doesn't want things like toys or games or a new bike. God's favorite gift is your praise!

Praising God means celebrating how good He is. And everyone's praise is different. Some people like to sing and dance to celebrate God, while others like to pray quietly. You can even praise God when things aren't going your way. When you celebrate God all the time, it shows that you love Him and believe that He will care for you. And that's the only gift God wants!

THOUGHT OF THE DAY

Giving God the gift of praise keeps you peaceful all your days!

PRAY TODAY

Dear God, You are so good all the time! Help me remember to praise You when I'm happy, sad, and everything in between. Amen.

COME BACK TO GOD

"Return to the LORD your God, for he is merciful and compassionate, slow to get angry and filled with unfailing love."

JOEL 2:13 NLT

Have you ever done or said something you wish you could take back? It happens to everyone! And it's not always easy to know what to do next.

Whenever you feel sorry or sad, talk to God. The Bible tells us that God doesn't get angry quickly and He is full of love. When you ask Him for forgiveness, He celebrates! He can't wait to gather you up in His arms and cover you with love. His love can give you courage to ask others for forgiveness too, and help make things right. There's nothing God's love can't do!

THOUGHT OF THE DAY

No matter what you do or where you go, you can always come back to God!

PRAY TODAY

Dear God, thank You for loving me so much. When I do something wrong, help me come back to You right away! Amen.

SPREAD CHEER

A cheerful heart is good medicine, but a broken spirit saps a person's strength.

PROVERBS 17:22 NLT

When you get sick, your mom or dad probably gives you medicine. Well, the Bible says that cheerfulness is like good medicine—it makes people feel better.

So how can you show cheerfulness? One way is to smile. And that can be contagious—most people will smile right back! Another way is to share kind words and deeds.

God loves it when we have a cheerful heart and share it with others. It lets them see the love and joy that God has given us.

THOUGHT OF THE DAY
Your smile can change someone's day!

PRAY TODAY
Dear God, thank You for giving me a cheerful heart and finding ways to give cheerfulness to others. Amen.

HELPFUL WORDS

LORD, help me control my tongue; help me be careful about what I say.

PSALM 141:3 NCV

There is a small part of your body that is very powerful. It is also hard to control. Can you guess what it is? It's your tongue!

Your tongue is so powerful because you use it to talk. And the words that come out of your mouth have the power to help people or to hurt them. Has someone ever said words that hurt your feelings? Have you ever said words that hurt someone else? We need God's help to make sure our words don't hurt others. Be sure to ask him to help you control your tongue each day!

THOUGHT OF THE DAY

How will you use your words to help someone today?

PRAY TODAY

Dear God, please help me remember that my words are important. Please help me to always use words that help. Amen.

HOW GOD SEES YOU

I will praise You because I have been remarkably and wonderfully made. Your works are wonderful, and I know this very well.

PSALM 139:14 HCSB

When we look at each other, we can see only what's outside. But when God looks at you, He sees inside your heart. He knows the things you love and the things you don't. He knows the things that make you nervous or excited or curious. He sees what makes you the uniquely wonderful kid He created. And He loves every part of you!

The book of Genesis says God made us in His image. That means you are a reflection of God! So thank Him when you look at yourself. You are a beautiful, important creation—inside and out!

THOUGHT OF THE DAY
God made only one you!

PRAY TODAY
Dear God, thank You that You see my outside and my inside. Help me remember that who I am is more important than what I look like. Amen.

BEING PATIENT

Always be humble and gentle. Be patient and accept each other with love.

EPHESIANS 4:2 ICB

Are you ever impatient? It's hard to wait for things you want. It's hard to not be able to do something the first time you try. It's hard to take turns. Patience is a way of showing others and ourselves that we don't always have to have our way.

When we let someone else go first, we are being patient. When we don't whine while waiting, we are being patient. When we give someone time to think, we are being patient. Being patient isn't always easy, but God says that when we are patient, we are showing love.

THOUGHT OF THE DAY

When have you been patient? What are some ways you can be more patient?

PRAY TODAY

Dear God, thank You for always being patient with me. Please help me be patient with other people too. Amen.

SMALL CHOICES, BIG CHANGES

Put on the new self, created to be like God in true righteousness and holiness.

EPHESIANS 4:24 NIV

Do you have habits? Some habits, like brushing your teeth or saying your prayers, are very good. But some habits can hurt you. Maybe it's easy to tell a lie, or you yell when you get angry. The good news is, God can help you change bad habits!

The Bible says that when we follow God, it's like we get a brand-new self. That means we can make brand-new choices because God is helping! And nothing is too hard for God. Just start today, and start small. One better choice every day can make a big difference.

THOUGHT OF THE DAY

What is something you'd like to do differently? How can you start today?

PRAY TODAY

Dear God, please help me make better choices every day. I want to have only good habits! Amen.

A GIFT FROM GOD

For by grace you have been saved through faith. And this is not your own doing; it is the gift of God.

EPHESIANS 2:8 ESV

Do you like presents? What's the best present you ever got? The Bible tells us about a wonderful gift God gives to each of His children. He gives us a place in His family forever!

God tells us all we have to do to receive this amazing gift is trust in Him and believe that He loves us. This is called *faith*. When you have faith in God, He promises to be with you always. Then you will never need to feel alone or afraid again. Isn't that the most wonderful gift you can imagine?

THOUGHT OF THE DAY

God's gifts are the best. Trust Him, and He'll take care of the rest!

PRAY TODAY

Dear God, thank You for giving me the gift of faith so I can trust in You and live with You forever. Amen.

GOD'S LOVE LASTS

You are my God, and I will praise you; you are my God, and I will exalt you. Give thanks to the LORD, for he is good; his love endures forever.

PSALM 118:28-29 NIV

Sometimes we get rid of things because they wear out, get old, or break. As you get bigger, you grow out of your clothes and even certain toys. But do you know what never changes? God's love for you!

God's love never wears out, gets old, or breaks. And you will never outgrow it! The Bible says, "His love endures forever." You can be sure that God's love for you will always be there. You can't do anything to lose it. So be sure to thank Him for His wonderful love that never changes.

THOUGHT OF THE DAY
God's love is forever!

PRAY TODAY
Dear God, thank You for always loving me and for never leaving me. Amen.

SHOW YOUR LOVE

There are three things that remain—faith, hope, and love—and the greatest of these is love.

1 CORINTHIANS 13:13 TLB

We often use the word "love" to say how we feel about something: "I love pizza!" or "I love my family." But when the Bible talks about love, it reminds us that love is more than a feeling. It's a way of acting. The Bible says love is patient, kind, loyal, not jealous, not bragging, not proud, not selfish or rude, and forgiving of others.

So real love, God's kind of love, is something we do. Every day you can look for ways to show love to your friends and family. Give it a try! Be creative about how you show love to others.

THOUGHT OF THE DAY

Can you name some ways others have shown their love to you? How can you show your love to someone else?

PRAY TODAY

Dear God, I want to show Your love to others. Will You help me find ways to do this every day? Amen.

DO THE WORK

"Solomon, you must understand this. The Lord has chosen you to build the Temple as his holy place. Be strong and finish the job."

1 CHRONICLES 28:10 ICB

When God told His people to build a giant temple, they were nervous. It was such a big job! What if they messed up? But King David told the workers that they should not be afraid to do the hard work. God would be right there helping them!

Have you ever had to do something hard? Learning how to play an instrument or a sport takes work. You may even feel nervous about making new friends. But keep going! God wants you to grow and learn, and He will give you strength and courage to do hard work. Just ask! You'll be amazed what you can do.

THOUGHT OF THE DAY

When you work with God, anything is possible.

PRAY TODAY

Dear God, sometimes I get discouraged when things aren't easy. Please help me to be strong and brave so I can learn new things! Amen.

DAY 258

WHAT CAN YOU DO?

"There's a youngster here with five barley loaves and a couple of fish! But what good is that with all this mob?"

JOHN 6:9 TLB

This Bible verse is about a time when a child gave Jesus his small lunch and Jesus multiplied it to make enough to feed thousands of people. Do you ever feel like you can't help others because you are just a child? If you ask Jesus to take what you *do* have and help you share it, He will. Maybe you can give some of your toys or books to children who don't have any. Maybe you can make a picture for someone who is lonely. Your small gift might make a BIG difference to someone! Ask Jesus how you can help. He will help you find a way.

THOUGHT OF THE DAY

Who needs your help today? What can you do?

PRAY TODAY

Dear God, thank You for giving me so much. Please help me to find ways to help others. Amen.

TOUGH FORGIVENESS

Never pay back evil with more evil. Do things in such a way that everyone can see that you are honorable.

ROMANS 12:17 NLT

Forgiveness isn't always easy. When someone hurts you, you may want to hurt them back! But God tells us to forgive, even when it's hard.

The Bible tells a story of two brothers named Jacob and Esau. Jacob stole from Esau, and then ran away from home! When Jacob came back years later, he was scared that Esau would hurt him. But Esau had forgiven Jacob long ago! He ran out to greet his brother with hugs and kisses and celebration. Because Esau chose forgiveness, Jacob was safe, and Esau had joy in his life. Forgiveness is good for everyone!

THOUGHT OF THE DAY

Do you feel angry toward someone? Ask God to help you forgive them!

PRAY TODAY

Dear God, I don't want to stay angry. Please teach me how to forgive so I can feel better and help others too. Amen.

TRUSTING GOD

When I am afraid, I will trust in You.

PSALM 56:3 HCSB

What do you do when you are afraid? God knows that sometimes we will be afraid, but He doesn't want us to feel alone. That's why He tells us to trust in Him. Trusting in God means believing that what He says is true and knowing His love will never go away. A good way to do this is to remember a Bible verse and to say it when we are afraid. Words from the Bible are true, and they help us remember that God is always with us. Can you memorize the verse above? Then the next time you are afraid, you can say it out loud!

THOUGHT OF THE DAY
God's Word is true and trustworthy.

PRAY TODAY
Dear God, thank You for being with me when I'm afraid. I'm so glad I can always trust in You. Amen.

KINDNESS STARTS WITH YOU

Therefore, as God's chosen people, holy and dearly loved, clothe yourselves with compassion, kindness, humility, gentleness and patience.

COLOSSIANS 3:12 NIV

Sometimes it's nice to let other people go before you. But God wants you to go first in one important thing: kindness!

The Bible tells us to think of kindness like putting on clothing. Everyone should be able to see it right away! When you choose to be nice first, you show people that you care about them. And you can be nice to *anyone*! So even if you think someone doesn't like you, or you don't know someone very well, you can take the first step. See what happens when kindness starts with you!

THOUGHT OF THE DAY

Pick someone to show kindness to today. Then be sure you go first!

PRAY TODAY

Dear God, please help kindness to be the first thing people notice about me! Amen.

WILLING TO FORGIVE

Make allowance for each other's faults, and forgive anyone who offends you. Remember, the Lord forgave you, so you must forgive others.

COLOSSIANS 3:13 NLT

Doesn't it feel great to know that God forgives you, no matter what? What a great gift!

Because forgiveness is so wonderful, God also wants us to forgive each other. That's not always easy—especially if your feelings still hurt or you're still angry. But God can help you. If you're having a hard time forgiving, think about a time you made a mistake. Then remember how God forgave you! Ask Him to make you willing to forgive. If you're ready to try, God is ready to help you.

THOUGHT OF THE DAY

If there's someone you need to forgive, talk things over with your parents too. They'd love to help!

PRAY TODAY

Dear God, please help me remember Your love and forgiveness when I need to forgive someone else. Amen.

COUNT YOUR BLESSINGS

Be happy with what you have. God has said, "I will never leave you or let you be alone."

HEBREWS 13:5B NLV

Have you ever wanted to feel happier? Here's a quick way to do that: count your blessings!

God's gifts in your life are called blessings. Some days, you might not feel like you have very many. But when you stop to count them, you might be surprised! Do you have a family you love? A silly friend who cracks you up? A cozy bed to snuggle in at night? When did you last eat something super delicious? Maybe you can run fast, climb high, or sing beautiful songs. Once you start naming all God's blessings, it's hard to stop. And it's even harder to feel sad!

THOUGHT OF THE DAY

The greatest blessing of all is God's love. And that's something you'll always have!

PRAY TODAY

Dear God, please help me remember all Your blessings. I want to be happy with all the things You've given me! Amen.

GOD'S HOUSE

"Be glad and rejoice, because your reward is great in heaven."

MATTHEW 5:12A HCSB

D o you love to invite friends over to your house? Isn't it fun to share what we have with the people we like? Jesus sure thinks so. That's why He wants us all to come over to His forever house: heaven! In fact, when you invite Jesus into your heart, He invites *you* to live with Him in heaven forever.

No one knows exactly what heaven will be like. But the Bible does tell us that there will be no more sadness or sickness, and you'll get to meet Jesus face to face. What a wonderful place to call home!

THOUGHT OF THE DAY

When you meet Jesus, what do you think you'll say to Him?

PRAY TODAY

Dear God, thank You for preparing such a wonderful forever home for me in heaven! Amen.

FRIENDS YOU CAN TRUST

Friends come and friends go, but a true friend sticks by you like family.

PROVERBS 18:24 MSG

Bob and Larry are best friends. They always tell the truth, and most importantly, they like each other just the way they are. A best friend is someone you can really depend on!

Do you want to have a friend like that? You can start by being one! Tell the truth kindly. Encourage one another. And never share gossip—about each other or anyone else.

Remember that true friends will like you for you. They won't try to change you. When you spend time with people like that, you'll find friends who feel like family!

THOUGHT OF THE DAY

Who are some of your friends? What do you like about them?

PRAY TODAY

Dear God, thank You for the friends You've given me. Please help me to be a trustworthy, loving friend to each one. Amen.

LOVING PATIENCE

Love is patient and kind.

1 CORINTHIANS 13:4A ESV

Has someone ever told you to be patient? Being patient doesn't just mean waiting. It means waiting *peacefully* and trusting that you will get what you need at the right time.

When you're patient around your parents, you show that you believe they love you and will take care of you. When you're patient with your friends, you show that you care about them and their ideas. And when you're patient with God, you show that you love Him and trust Him to care for you. Patience isn't always easy, but it's a great way to show love!

THOUGHT OF THE DAY

Patience comes with practice. Find two ways to practice patience today!

PRAY TODAY

Dear God, I know You want what's best for me. Help me to be patient with You and with my friends and family. Amen.

LOOK FOR GOODNESS

The one who searches for what is good finds favor, but if someone looks for trouble, it will come to him.

PROVERBS 11:27 HCSB

If you want to find something, what do you do? You look for it!

Do you want to find good things? They are everywhere! Look for goodness in everyone you meet. Notice the beautiful songs that birds sing or the delicious smell of dinner cooking. Search for something happy in everything that happens. Even bad days have some good hidden in them.

If you spend your time focusing on things that make you sad or angry, that's all you'll see. Instead, look for good! God can help you find exactly what you need.

THOUGHT OF THE DAY

What are three good things that happened today?

PRAY TODAY

Dear God, You made such a good world! Please help me look for goodness all day every day! Amen.

GOD'S PERFECT LOVE

For though we have never yet seen God, when we love each other God lives in us, and his love within us grows ever stronger.

1 JOHN 4:12 TLB

Do you know that God's perfect love lives in you? The Bible says God lives in all His children so that they grow up in His love.

Just as God shares His love with you, He wants you to share His love with His other children too. That's how you show you're growing up in God's perfect love. When you love other people, you show them God's love at the same time. Look around and see who might need love today. Then use kind words and deeds to let them know that God loves them too!

THOUGHT OF THE DAY
Who can you surprise with God's love today?

PRAY TODAY
Dear God, thank You for loving me so much. Please help me share Your love with others every day. Amen.

@ @ @ @ @ @ @

CHOOSING HOPE

Let your unfailing love surround us, LORD, for our hope is in you alone.

PSALM 33:22 NLT

God loves you, and He has big plans for you. You can be sure that's true because He says so in the Bible! But there will be days when you feel like nothing is going the way you want. Those are great times to practice hope. Hope is one of God's greatest gifts! It means being sure that God is in control, even when you can't see how everything will work out. Choose hope by choosing to trust God's promises. If it's hard to trust, ask for His help! God wants you to live hopefully and confidently. He will never let you down.

THOUGHT OF THE DAY
When you live with hope, you live with joy!

PRAY TODAY
Dear God, thank You for the gift of hope. Please help me trust Your love and guidance! Amen.

ANYTHING IS POSSIBLE!

Jesus said to him . . . "Everything is possible to the one who believes."

MARK 9:23 HCSB

Have you ever wanted to do something hard? Maybe you're learning something new—like playing a sport or learning to draw. Maybe you're trying to make friends at a new school. God has good news for you. He can help you do anything!

God loves to help His children do great things. So ask for His help! It may be hard work, but you won't be doing it alone. Anytime you feel frustrated, ask Him to give you strength. If you feel nervous, ask for His peace. God is on your side. He will never let you down.

THOUGHT OF THE DAY

What can God help you do today?

PRAY TODAY

Dear God, I'm so happy that nothing is too hard for You! Please help me work hard and remember that You are always with me. Amen.

NEVER GIVE UP

We can rejoice, too, when we run into problems and trials, for we know that they are good for us—they help us learn to be patient. And patience develops strength of character in us and helps us trust God more each time we use it until finally our hope and faith are strong and steady.

ROMANS 5:3–4 TLB

Sometimes when things are hard to do, we might feel like giving up. But if we quit, we won't learn how to do them. If you gave up trying you might never learn to do important things like write your name or count or ride your bike or make friends. The Bible says it is good to keep trying when things are hard because that helps us grow. Remember, you're not in this alone. God will always help us learn new things if we don't give up!

THOUGHT OF THE DAY

Trying hard is the thing to do when you're learning something new!

PRAY TODAY

Dear God, thank You for helping me to grow. Please help me to keep trying even when things are hard to do. Amen.

KIND THOUGHTS

A wise person is patient. He will be honored if he ignores a wrong done against him.

PROVERBS 19:11 ICB

God tells us to forgive each other. That means we don't repay meanness with meanness. But it also means changing the way we think about the person who hurt us.

It's easy to think kind thoughts about people who make us happy. But what about when someone makes you angry or sad? God still wants you to think kindly about them. Don't sit around and feel angry. Instead, pray for them. You can even ask God to bless them. Remember that everyone makes mistakes. When you stop being angry and start thinking kind thoughts again, that's true forgiveness!

THOUGHT OF THE DAY

Forgiveness takes patience and practice. Keep asking God for help!

PRAY TODAY

Dear God, forgiveness can be hard. Please help me think only kind thoughts. Amen.

ALWAYS PEACEFUL

Now may the Lord of peace himself give you peace at all times in every way. The Lord be with you all.

2 THESSALONIANS 3:16 ESV

Feeling peaceful means you feel calm and certain that everything is OK. What a great way to feel! And the Bible says with God, we can feel peaceful all the time. God gives us peace through His great big love. It's a love that sticks around in good times and hard times. And like His love, God never changes! He is always strong, always powerful, and He always keeps His promises. So if you ever feel sad or scared or angry, remember God. He is right here, waiting to give you His wonderful peace!

THOUGHT OF THE DAY

Every day is different, but God is always the same!

PRAY TODAY

Dear God, when I feel worried or angry or sad, please help me remember Your love. Help me feel peaceful every day. Amen.

TURN ON THE LIGHTS!

Walk as children of light (for the fruit of light is found in all that is good and right and true).

EPHESIANS 5:8B–9 ESV

Have you ever seen Christmas lights on a house? At night, the tiny lights shine brightly for everyone to see. It's hard not to feel joyful around Christmas lights!

Having Jesus in your heart is like having Christmas lights up all the time! Jesus can fill your heart with joy and peace, no matter what happens. And He shows you how to make good choices so you can be a great friend and help others. So when you walk through your day, remember to turn on your lights! You'll share joy with everyone you meet.

THOUGHT OF THE DAY

Others may want to know how they can shine brightly too. Tell them that it's all from Jesus!

PRAY TODAY

Dear God, thank You that Jesus can live in my heart and light me up from the inside out! Amen.

@ @ @ @ @ @ @

HARD TIMES

"If you'll hold on to me for dear life," says GOD, "I'll get you out of any trouble. I'll give you the best of care if you'll only get to know and trust me. Call me and I'll answer, be at your side in bad times."

PSALM 91:14–15A MSG

Have you ever had a really hard day? Maybe things didn't go your way, or you kept getting in trouble. Maybe you felt angry or sad, and couldn't figure out how to feel better. Guess what? God is with you, even in those really hard times.

God gives us a great promise: If we stay close to Him, He can get us through anything. When you trust God, He holds your hand every day. And He's always listening when you pray. So reach out for Him! He is waiting to lead you through every day, in good times and bad.

THOUGHT OF THE DAY

God is a wonderful friend!

PRAY TODAY

Dear God, thank You for never leaving my side. Please remind me to talk to You when I have hard days. Amen.

THE BEST THINGS

Don't be obsessed with getting more material things. Be relaxed with what you have.

HEBREWS 13:5 MSG

Do you ever want more stuff? Maybe a friend has a toy that you wish you had. It's normal to want things. But when wanting becomes all you think about, that's called jealousy. And jealousy doesn't feel good.

God wants you to think about what you do have instead of what you don't have, like the toys you love to play with or your favorite bedtime book. But most important, think about everyone who loves you—including God! Family, friends, and God's love are the very best things you can ever have.

THOUGHT OF THE DAY

When you start to feel jealous, try naming three things you already have that make you happy!

PRAY TODAY

Dear God, You have given me really good gifts. Help me remember them instead of wanting what someone else has! Amen.

MAKE FEAR DISAPPEAR

There is no fear in love, but perfect love casts out fear.

1 JOHN 4:18 ESV

Did you know that God is love? When God is with you, you have love inside you. The Bible tells us that "perfect love casts out fear." That means that when we are filled with God's love, there's no room left for fear.

The next time you feel afraid, think about God's love for you. Remember that He is always with you and that He is greater and more powerful than any of your fears. As you think more about God's great love, your fears will get smaller and smaller. And soon, they will be gone!

THOUGHT OF THE DAY

God's great love makes fear disappear!

PRAY TODAY

Dear God, thank You for Your perfect love that is more powerful than my fears. Amen.

LOOK ON THE BRIGHT SIDE

A happy heart makes the face cheerful, but heartache crushes the spirit.

PROVERBS 15:13 NIV

Have you ever had a day when everything was going great? How about a day when everything seemed to go wrong? The Bible says that if we have a happy heart, we can enjoy life—even when our day isn't going the way we want.

If the rain spoils your picnic, you can splash in the puddles! What if your friend can't come over to play? Maybe you can make up a new game with your toys. Instead of getting angry when things go wrong, find something to be glad about. That's called looking on the bright side!

THOUGHT OF THE DAY

How can you look on the bright side the next time things don't go the way you want?

PRAY TODAY

Dear God, I know bad things happen sometimes. When they do, please help me to look on the bright side. Amen.

WORDS ARE GIFTS

Say only what helps, each word a gift.

EPHESIANS 4:29B MSG

Did you know that your words can be a gift to someone? Your words can help someone who is having a hard time. They can cheer up someone who is sad. Kind words can let someone know you love them.

Maybe someone needs to hear "I care about you." Or perhaps they need to hear "How can I help?" Did you know that "I'm sorry" and "I will pray for you" are also words that show kindness? If you don't know what to say, just ask God to give you helpful words. Make your words a gift to someone today!

THOUGHT OF THE DAY

When friends or family need a lift, your helpful words can be a gift!

PRAY TODAY

Dear God, please help me use my words as gifts of kindness and love. Amen.

SING FOR JOY

Shout with joy to the LORD, all the earth! Worship the LORD with gladness. Come before him, singing with joy.

PSALM 100:1-2 NLT

What do you do when you are really happy? Do you jump up and down? Sing a song? Wave your arms and laugh? It's hard to keep joy inside, isn't it?

The Bible tells us about a great king named David who wrote songs, played the harp, and shouted for joy when he was happy. David knew that God loves to hear His people praise Him and sing to Him when they are happy. God created us to find joy in life, and He loves it when we share that joy with others too!

THOUGHT OF THE DAY

What are some ways you can think of to show God you are filled with joy?

PRAY TODAY

Dear God, thank You for loving me and giving me so many things to be happy about. Amen.

NEW FRIENDS ARE EVERYWHERE!

When you're kind to others, you help yourself; when you're cruel to others, you hurt yourself.

PROVERBS 11:17 MSG

Do you want to make new friends? Good news! New friends are everywhere! All you have to do is be kind. You can share what you have, invite someone new to play a game, and say encouraging words. Kindness is the best way to make new friends.

If someone starts at a new school or moves to a new neighborhood, making friends can seem like a big job. Ask God to show you ways to be kind to the new kids you meet. When you are friendly to others, they'll almost always want to act the same way!

THOUGHT OF THE DAY

The best way to make a friend is to be a friend!

PRAY TODAY

Dear God, I don't always know how to make new friends. Please help me start with kindness! Amen.

A QUIET TIME

I wait quietly before God, for my hope is in him.

PSALM 62:5 NLT

Do you love being with friends? Because Jesus wants to be your good friend, He loves when you choose to spend time with Him too. But how do you spend time with a friend you can't see?

Some people set aside a few minutes each day for a quiet time with God. They might pray, read Bible verses, sing songs about God, or just be still and wait for God's thoughts to come to their mind. Spending time with a friend is how you get to know each other better. Spending time with God works the same way!

THOUGHT OF THE DAY

When can you spend some quiet time with Jesus today?

PRAY TODAY

Dear God, I want to know You better. Please help me find time to be quiet with You today. Amen.

PRAY FOR EVERYONE

First of all, I ask you to pray for everyone. Ask God to help and bless them all, and tell God how thankful you are for each of them.

1 TIMOTHY 2:1 CEV

Talking to God is a powerful thing. So why not use that power to help others? Praying for other people is one of the best ways to care for them. If you know them well, you can pray for something you know they need. Or just give thanks for the people in your life, and ask God to bless them. You can even pray for people you've never met! God loves everyone, and we all need His help—from your best friend to the president. Prayer may seem like a small thing. But it's a super important job!

THOUGHT OF THE DAY

Make a list of five people to pray for every day. Try to include at least one person you don't know!

PRAY TODAY

Dear God, I'm so glad You love all of us. Please help me show Your love to everyone I meet today. Amen.

JESUS LOVES YOU

"As the Father has loved Me, I have also loved you. Remain in My love."

JOHN 15:9 HCSB

Do you know the song "Jesus Loves Me"? It goes: "Jesus loves me this I know, for the Bible tells me so!" It is a simple song, but it contains one of the most amazing facts you'll ever know: Jesus loves you!

That is amazing because Jesus created the whole universe and everything in it. He made stars and planets, gigantic mountains and seas, and tiny bugs and birds. And He loves you! You are very special to God. So, whenever you feel lonely or sad, remember that Jesus, who made the whole world, loves you!

THOUGHT OF THE DAY

God's Word is always right and true, so you can trust that God loves you!

PRAY TODAY

Dear God, thank You for loving me always, no matter what. Amen.

SPECIAL GIFTS

Something from the Spirit can be seen in each person, to help everyone.

1 CORINTHIANS 12:7 ICB

God has given each of us special gifts. And they're all different! What's even cooler is that each gift can be used to help other people. If you love to draw, you can make pretty cards for a sick friend. If you're great at sports, you can help other kids learn how to play. If you love books, why not read to a younger sibling? Do you love animals? Offer to walk your neighbor's dog! Your gifts are wonderful. Share them with the world!

THOUGHT OF THE DAY

What's something you love to do?

PRAY TODAY

Dear God, thank You for all the things I love to do. Help me use my gifts to help others! Amen.

GOOD MEDICINE

A cheerful heart is good medicine, but a broken spirit saps a person's strength.

PROVERBS 17:22 NLT

If you get an earache or you have a bad cough, the doctor might give you medicine to help you get better. Did you know that there is a special kind of medicine that you can give your friends who are feeling sad or lonely? The Bible says, "A cheerful heart is good medicine"! That's because sharing a smile, a laugh, or even a hug reminds others that you care about them. And that makes anyone feel great! A gift of cheer is good medicine. And you don't even have to go to the doctor!

THOUGHT OF THE DAY

Can you think of someone who needs some cheering up? What can you do for them today?

PRAY TODAY

Dear God, please help me find ways to help someone feel better today. Amen.

SAY NO TO GOSSIP

Without wood, a fire will go out, and without gossip, quarreling will stop.

PROVERBS 26:20 NCV

Have you ever met someone who likes to say mean things about others? Maybe they want you to do the same thing. But don't do it! It's called *gossip*, and it can hurt people. Instead, always choose to say good things about others—even when they aren't around.

You might feel tempted to gossip because you think people will like you more. But those aren't the kinds of friendships God wants you to have. Spreading unkind words—true or untrue—can really hurt feelings. If someone asks you to tell a secret or complain about someone, just say no. Then say something kind instead!

THOUGHT OF THE DAY
Never say anything about someone that you wouldn't tell them face to face!

PRAY TODAY
Dear God, please help me choose encouraging words instead of gossip. And help me make friends who do the same! Amen.

DON'T FORGET THE TRUTH

Don't ever forget kindness and truth. Wear them like a necklace. Write them on your heart as if on a tablet.

PROVERBS 3:3 NCV

Can you think of a time when it was hard to tell the truth? Maybe you felt embarrassed, or you were afraid you'd get in trouble. But God tells us that telling the truth with kindness is always the right choice. So how do we do that when it's hard? We make sure we're always ready!

The Bible says to carry the truth around all the time. When you're honest about little things, it'll be easier to be honest about big things too. So don't forget to bring truth and kindness with you wherever you go!

THOUGHT OF THE DAY

Truth and kindness are best friends.

PRAY TODAY

Dear God, please help me tell the truth with kindness everywhere I go. Amen.

GOD ALWAYS FORGIVES

If we tell Him our sins, He is faithful and we can depend on Him to forgive us of our sins. He will make our lives clean from all sin.

1 JOHN 1:9 NLV

Do you ever have one of those days (or weeks!) where you feel like you keep getting in trouble? Sometimes it's hard to make good choices! But here's some good news: God never gets tired of forgiving you. Whenever we tell God our sins and ask Him to forgive us, He does it right away. It's a wonderful promise!

Remember that no one is perfect. But God's love for you will never change. He is always with you and always ready to forgive!

THOUGHT OF THE DAY

Every day is a fresh new start!

PRAY TODAY

Dear God, thank You for promising to forgive me every time I ask. Help me make better choices tomorrow. Amen.

WHAT'S GOOD FOR YOU

I can do anything I want to if Christ has not said no, but some of these things aren't good for me.

1 CORINTHIANS 6:12A TLB

Habits are things you do all the time. Some habits help you, but some can hurt. How can you know which is which?

Remember that the Bible tells us that we should only do things that are kind to others and ourselves. Think of what you do each day. Maybe you pray before meals. That's a good habit! It brings you closer to God. Do you bite your nails or suck your thumb? Those aren't good habits because they can harm your body. Habits are hard to change, but God can help you choose what's good for you!

THOUGHT OF THE DAY

To start a new good habit, do it at the same time every day.

PRAY TODAY

Dear God, please show me which habits are good and which need to change. I can do anything with Your help! Amen.

GOD LIKES YOU

"For the LORD your God is living among you. He is a mighty savior. He will take delight in you with gladness. With his love, he will calm all your fear. He will rejoice over you with joyful songs."

ZEPHANIAH 3:17 NLT

Who is someone you love to spend time with? Your mom and dad? A special aunt? A best friend? Think of how you feel about that person—that's how God feels about you! God thinks you are super cool, and He really enjoys hanging out with you. Your ideas are interesting to Him. He loves to hear your questions, and your stories make Him smile. The Bible says He likes you so much, He even sings happy songs about you! Nothing makes God happier than spending time with a great friend: you!

THOUGHT OF THE DAY

What's something you and your friends talk about? Share it with God too!

PRAY TODAY

Dear God, I'm so glad we're friends! Thank You for loving and liking me so much! Amen.

BE A HERO

Now if you really obey the LORD . . . God will set you high above all nations on earth.

DEUTERONOMY 28:1 CEB

Who are your favorite Bible heroes? Larry loves the story of Joshua, who trusted some pretty weird instructions from God and won a huge battle! Pa Grape likes the story of Esther, an ordinary girl who became queen and risked her life to save her people.

All Bible heroes have one thing in common: they obeyed God. When you obey God, He promises to bless you. And His blessings may surprise you! You might not become a queen or a famous soldier, but you'll be a hero for God!

THOUGHT OF THE DAY

How can you obey God today?

PRAY TODAY

Dear God, please help me obey You, even when it's hard. I want to be a hero for You! Amen.

HOW TO LOVE GOD

This is love for God: to keep his commands.

1 JOHN 5:3 NIV

The Bible tells us that there's a simple way to show God you love Him: obey Him. But those simple directions aren't always easy to follow! Do you ever have a hard time obeying God? We all do sometimes. But here's some good news: God is always ready to forgive. In fact, asking for forgiveness means you're obeying one of God's commands! So keep trying to obey God. And if you make a mistake, just ask for forgiveness and try again! When you show God you want to follow His commands, He knows you love and trust Him.

THOUGHT OF THE DAY

When is it hardest to obey God? Ask Him to help you try extra hard at those moments!

PRAY TODAY

Dear God, I want to obey You. Thank You for giving me lots of chances to try again! Amen.

WHAT'S YOUR STORY?

All who worship God, come here and listen; I will tell you everything God has done for me.

PSALM 66:16 CEV

If you know God, then you have a story to tell! Has God ever answered one of your prayers? Has He helped you be brave when you were afraid? Has He helped you get better when you were sick? When someone wonders about who God is and what He does, tell your story. You can talk about how God loves everyone. You can share how He listens to prayers and answers them. You can tell a story about one of the ways He helped you. When you tell your story, you help others to know and trust God.

THOUGHT OF THE DAY

What story will you tell about God?

PRAY TODAY

Dear God, thank You for all the many things You have done for me. Please help me share my story with my friends. Amen.

A JOYFUL GIVER

God loves the person who gives happily.

2 CORINTHIANS 9:7B ICB

Do you like going to birthday parties? It's so much fun to play games and eat yummy treats. But when you spend time choosing just the right birthday present for your friend, you probably feel most excited for her to open it. That's how God wants you to feel anytime you give something to someone else!

You can give special gifts whenever you want to. Make a card for a sick family member. Share your lunch with a friend who forgot his. Give your time by helping others. Try to figure out what someone else would most like or need. Then be happy to give it!

THOUGHT OF THE DAY

When you give with a happy heart, everyone gets something special!

PRAY TODAY

Dear God, please make me a happy giver. It's fun to get presents, but I want to be excited to give them too! Amen.

DO IT GOD'S WAY!

But Jesus said, "Those who hear the teaching of God and obey it—they are the ones who are truly blessed."

LUKE 11:28 ICB

The Bible tells the amazing story of a man named Joshua. God told Joshua to lead His people into the city of Jericho. But there was a huge wall around the city to keep out armies like Joshua's. God didn't say to climb over it or tear it down. Instead, He said the army should march around the city seven times and then blow their trumpets and shout. That's it! It sounded strange, but Joshua convinced everyone to obey God. When they did exactly what God said, the walls crumbled and fell! That day, everyone saw that obeying God is always the best idea.

THOUGHT OF THE DAY

Obey God, even if His directions seem strange.
Then watch what amazing things He does!

PRAY TODAY

Dear God, help me trust Your directions, even when I think I have a better idea. Amen.

ⓔ ⓢ ⓔ ⓢ ⓢ ⓔ ⓔ ⓢ

HOW TO FIND GOD

"But from there you will search for the LORD your God, and you will find Him when you seek Him with all your heart and all your soul."

DEUTERONOMY 4:29 HCSB

Have you ever played hide-and-seek with a friend? You close your eyes and count while your friend hides, and then you say, "Ready or not, here I come!" Then you look everywhere you can think of to find your friend. God makes it easy for us to find Him anytime we want! All we have to do is *want* to find Him. We can read about Him in our Bibles. We can hear about Him at church. We can talk to Him any time we want. God never hides from us. He always wants us to find Him.

THOUGHT OF THE DAY

How do you look for God?

PRAY TODAY

Dear God, thank You for always being near and for making it easy for me to find You anytime I want. Amen.

BE A HAPPY HELPER

Do everything without complaining and arguing.

PHILIPPIANS 2:14 NLT

God wants us to be happy helpers. That means we should follow directions right away and without arguing.

When a parent or teacher asks you to do something, you have a choice. You can say, "Sure! I can do that!" Or you can say, "Aw, do I have to?" Which do you think would make God glad?

Following directions the first time we are asked makes everyone happier. It also shows that we are doing what God wants us to do—helping without complaining. So next time your mom or dad asks you to do something, put on a smile and be a happy helper!

THOUGHT OF THE DAY

Smile first, then respond. That's the first step to being a happy helper!

PRAY TODAY

Dear God, sometimes it's hard to follow directions. Please help me stay away from arguing so I can be happy instead. Amen!

BEST FRIEND FOREVER

And I am convinced that nothing can ever separate us from God's love. . . . No power in the sky above or in the earth below—indeed, nothing in all creation will ever be able to separate us from the love of God that is revealed in Christ Jesus our Lord.

ROMANS 8:38–39 NLT

Jesus loves you so much. In fact, there is nowhere you can go to get away from His love! When you feel lonely, Jesus is still with you. You may go through times when following God is extra hard, but Jesus is still there. You may even get mad at God sometimes, but He won't go anywhere! He's your best friend forever.

When you invite Jesus to live in your life, He comes to stay. Isn't it great to know your very best friend will never leave you?

THOUGHT OF THE DAY

Can you think of a Bible story that shows Jesus' love for us?

PRAY TODAY

Dear God, thank You for Your great big love! I want Jesus to be my best friend forever! Amen.

TWO LITTLE WORDS

Admit your faults . . . and pray for each other so that you may be healed.

JAMES 5:16 TLB

Why is it so hard to apologize sometimes? Maybe you feel proud and don't want to admit that you were wrong. Maybe you feel embarrassed. Maybe you're worried you'll get in trouble. But be brave! Two of the most powerful words you can ever say are "I'm sorry." Those words can heal hurt feelings. And they can build really strong friendships! So don't be afraid of saying you're sorry. Do it right away, and watch what God does with those two little words!

THOUGHT OF THE DAY

Even if what happened was an accident, it's important to say you're sorry. Then the healing can begin!

PRAY TODAY

Dear God, thank You that You always forgive me. Help me say "I'm sorry" to others and ask for their forgiveness too. Amen.

YOUR BEST FRIEND

"You are my friends if you obey me. Servants don't know what their master is doing, and so I don't speak to you as servants. I speak to you as my friends, and I have told you everything that my Father has told me."

JOHN 15:14–15 CEV

Do you have a best friend? Best friends help each other. They always stick up for one another. They care about one another and spend time together having fun. Guess what? Jesus wants to be your best friend! He will always help you and care for you. He always tells you the truth, and He never leaves you all alone. When we do what Jesus says to do, we show that Jesus is our best friend too. Isn't it great to have a best friend like Jesus?

THOUGHT OF THE DAY

Be sure to talk with Jesus every day! Talking together is how friends become *best* friends.

PRAY TODAY

Dear God, thank You for being my very best friend. I love You, and I want to be a good friend to You too! Amen.

LOVE YOUR ENEMY

"There is a saying, 'Love your friends and hate your enemies.' But I say: Love your enemies! Pray for those who persecute you!"

MATTHEW 5:43–44 TLB

Jesus says some pretty surprising things. But maybe the most surprising is "love your enemies!" Why should we love people we don't even like very much? Especially if they aren't nice to us!

Jesus knows that selfless love can change anything. It can help lonely people feel cared for. It can calm someone's anger. It can introduce someone to God. It can even turn enemies into friends. When you have the chance to show love to someone, always do it. It can be as easy as a kind word or a shared snack. You never know what will happen!

THOUGHT OF THE DAY

Is there someone you know who is hard to love? How can you love them today?

PRAY TODAY

Dear God, You love everyone. Help me love everyone too. Amen.

SURPRISE!

The L{ORD} your God is God of all gods and Lord of all lords. He is the great God, who is strong and wonderful.

DEUTERONOMY 10:17A NCV

The Bible is full of stories where God surprises people with wonderful blessings. Esther became queen even though she was never part of a royal family. The Israelites destroyed the walls of a huge city just by blasting trumpets. Mary got to be Jesus' mother!

God still loves to amaze us. When you trust God, incredible things can happen. You can make great friends in a new place. You can feel joyful even when bad things happen. God can give you ideas you'd never think of on your own. That's why it's important to pray and read your Bible each day. You never know what God might do!

THOUGHT OF THE DAY

The Bible says God is strong and wonderful. He's also surprising!

PRAY TODAY

Dear God, I'm so glad You can do anything. I can't wait to see what You do today! Amen.

PEACE FOR FREE

"Peace I leave with you; my peace I give you. I do not give to you as the world gives."

JOHN 14:27A NIV

If you want something from a store, you need to pay for it. But if you want peace from God, all you have to do is ask! It's ready any time you want it, and it doesn't cost a penny.

If you want to know what God's peace looks like, just get to know Him better! Pray and read your Bible every day. Memorize Bible verses, and share Bible stories with people you know. When you're close to God, you'll start to notice all the ways He blesses you and answers your prayers. He loves to give you peace!

THOUGHT OF THE DAY

When you spend time with God, His peace comes along too!

PRAY TODAY

Dear God, thanks for giving me Your peace for free! I am so glad You share good gifts with me. Amen.

DOING LOVE

My children, our love should not be only words and talk. Our love must be true love. And we should show that love by what we do.

1 JOHN 3:18 ICB

Many people think that love is a feeling. But the Bible says that love is something we do. If we say we love someone, but we don't act in loving ways, then we are not telling the truth. If a friend is sad, you can show your love by listening to him or her and spending time together. If your parents ask you to help at home, you can show them your love by helping without complaining. It is good to tell others that we love them, but the Bible says that *doing* love is even better!

THOUGHT OF THE DAY

Try to think of three different ways to "do love" today.

PRAY TODAY

Dear God, thank You for loving me. Help me show my love to others by doing kind, patient, and caring things for them. Amen.

THE TRUTH IS KIND

Since you put away lying, Speak the truth, each one to his neighbor, because we are members of one another.

EPHESIANS 4:25 HCSB

Have you ever felt like telling a lie? Sometimes it's hard to tell the truth! But God says that we should always be honest. That's because honesty is kind. Truthful people play fair, admit when they are wrong, and speak up when they see others getting hurt. Doesn't that sound like a good friend?

Telling the truth is always the right thing to do. It's not always easy, but you're not alone! Ask God to help you speak truthfully, so you can be kind and loving—just the way He made you to be!

THOUGHT OF THE DAY

God is the truth expert—He always tells us the truth!

PRAY TODAY

Dear God, help me remember that telling the truth is the kind choice. I'm so glad everything You say is true! Amen.

HELPING HANDS

Never walk away from someone who deserves help; your hand is God's hand for that person.

PROVERBS 3:27 MSG

Look at your hands. Notice anything special about them? Well, when you help others, your hands become God's hands!

Your hands can do so many things. They can draw a picture for a relative who lives far away. They can lift up a friend who's fallen down. They can give big hugs to celebrate big wins! And they can hold someone else's hand to offer a little extra support and strength. With God by your side, you can make a difference to someone—or lots of someones! What will your hands do today?

THOUGHT OF THE DAY

Jesus blesses little hands that lovingly fulfill His plans.

PRAY TODAY

Dear God, I'm so glad my little hands can do big things! Please show me how I can help someone today. Amen.

GOD HEARS YOU

But God did listen! He paid attention to my prayer. Praise God, who did not ignore my prayer or withdraw his unfailing love from me.

PSALM 66:19–20 NLT

God promises He will always listen to your prayers. And He'll always answer you. But His answers may not always be what you expect.

Try this experiment at home: Make a list of things you want to pray about. Maybe it's feeling comfortable in a new school. Maybe you need help learning a skill, following the rules, or speaking up when something's wrong. Maybe you just want to feel closer to God! Pray every day, and once every week, check in with the list. You may be surprised by how God chose to answer your prayers!

THOUGHT OF THE DAY
The things you care about matter to God!

PRAY TODAY
Dear God, thank You for always hearing my prayers. I know You will answer when I talk to You! Amen.

HEAVEN IS WONDERFUL

"No eye has seen, no ear has heard, and no mind has imagined what God has prepared for those who love him."

1 CORINTHIANS 2:9B NLT

Do you wonder what heaven is like? The Bible uses picture language to tell us about it, saying the streets are gold, the light is like jewels, and there is beautiful music that sounds like rushing water. It also says there will be no sadness or sickness in heaven.

But those are just hints. Scripture tells us that heaven is more wonderful than we can even imagine! Because God loves us, He has prepared an amazing home where we will live with Him forever. You can be sure of one thing about heaven—it will be even better than you think!!

THOUGHT OF THE DAY

Heaven is real . . . and it's even more amazing than you can imagine!

PRAY TODAY

Dear God, thank You for making heaven where I can live with You forever. Amen.

GOD'S THOUGHTS

Let God change the way you think. Then you will know how to do everything that is good and pleasing to him.

ROMANS 12:2 CEV

It's sometimes hard to make the right choice—especially if everyone around you is doing something different. But God can help!

Ask God to help you focus on things that please Him. We know He loves words that help instead of hurt. He's happy when we share what we have with others. He sees good in everyone. When you fix your mind on what is important to God, He can help you make hard decisions. You may be the only one who chooses what God wants, but that's just fine. Who knows? Others might even follow your lead!

THOUGHT OF THE DAY

Good thoughts lead to good actions!

PRAY TODAY

Dear God, please help me to be strong and make the right choice, even if it feels like I'm the only one! Amen.

@ @ @ @ @ @ @

AN HONEST EXAMPLE

In every way be an example of doing good deeds. When you teach, do it with honesty and seriousness.

TITUS 2:7 NCV

Do you have teachers you like? Guess what? You can be a teacher too! When you choose to tell the truth and act honestly, you're being a good example. That's just like teaching others how to behave!

Telling the truth can be hard. But when others see you choosing to be honest, they'll learn that they can do it too. And they'll learn that you're a good friend they can trust. So think carefully about how you choose to act. You could inspire someone else!

THOUGHT OF THE DAY

Honesty isn't just about you. It also helps the people you're truthful to!

PRAY TODAY

Dear God, please help me choose honesty, so I can be a good example to my friends and family. Amen.

PLENTY TO SHARE

And God will generously provide all you need. Then you will always have everything you need and plenty left over to share with others.

2 CORINTHIANS 9:8 NLT

God has promised to give us everything we need. But do you ever forget that? Sometimes it's hard to trust God. We might think we need more and more stuff to make us happy. But that's not true!

One way to get back to trusting God is to share what you have with others. Do you have a coat that's too small? Give it to a younger friend or sibling. What about books you don't read anymore? Can you donate them to your school? The more you give, the more you'll realize that God's given you all you need. In fact, He's given you plenty to share as well!

THOUGHT OF THE DAY

Choose one thing today that you can give away to someone who needs it.

PRAY TODAY

Dear God, please help me remember that You will give me everything I need. Then help me share with others! Amen.

YOU'VE GOT THIS!

"Don't worry about this Philistine," David told Saul. "I'll go fight him!"

1 SAMUEL 17:32 NLT

The Bible tells a story of a young boy named David who fought a huge warrior named Goliath. Everyone in the Israelite army was too afraid to fight Goliath, but David said, "I'll do it!" David wasn't even a soldier! But because he trusted God and used the talents God gave him, David won.

Hopefully, you'll never fight a giant! But maybe you have to do something else that takes courage, like perform in front of lots of people, or go to a new school. When something is scary, trust God to help you. He can make you brave like David!

THOUGHT OF THE DAY

God wants you to try big things. Trust in Him and the courage He brings!

PRAY TODAY

Dear God, sometimes I just don't want to do scary things. Help me trust in You, just like David did. Amen.

GOD'S PERFECT LOVE

No one has ever seen God; if we love one another, God abides in us and his love is perfected in us.

1 JOHN 4:12 ESV

Do you know anyone who never does anything wrong? Of course not! The Bible says no one is perfect except for God. But we CAN be part of God's perfection!

When you love others, God's love is made perfect in you. That means God's love grows bigger inside you— which means more for you and more to share! It also means your love will start to look like God's. Using helpful words, showing patience, listening to others' ideas, and welcoming new friends are all ways you can show God's love. You don't have to be perfect. But God's love can be perfected in you!

THOUGHT OF THE DAY

What are some ways you can show God's love today?

PRAY TODAY

Dear God, I am so glad that You are perfect. Please make Your love perfect in me each day. Amen.

@ @ @ @ @ @ @

SMALL ACTIONS, BIG IMPACT

"For the Son of Man is going to come with His angels in the glory of His Father, and then He will reward each according to what he has done."

MATTHEW 16:27 HCSB

You might feel too little to make a big difference. But guess what? Every day you have lots of chances to make someone's day brighter.

Even small actions can have a big impact. Think about when someone has been kind to you. How does it feel to get a hug on a bad day or to laugh at a friend's silly story when you're feeling lonely? When you do kind things for others, you make them feel loved and encouraged. God has given you the ability to love people. So find ways to show that love each and every day!

THOUGHT OF THE DAY

Choose three small ways to love people today. Even a smile can go a long way!

PRAY TODAY

Dear God, please show me how I can make a difference to someone today. Amen.

WHAT'S HAPPENING?

"I know that You can do all things. Nothing can put a stop to Your plans."

JOB 42:2 NLV

Do you ever wonder about what is going to happen in the future? What you'll be when you grow up? If you'll have great adventures?

Because we are human, we don't know the future. But there is one thing we can be sure about: God knows all about it. God has good plans, and nothing can stop them. When you wonder about how things will turn out, remember to pray and thank God that His good plans will come to pass. You can rest, knowing that God is in control of today—and tomorrow too!

THOUGHT OF THE DAY

You may not know the future, but you can know it is in God's hands.

PRAY TODAY

Dear God, I'm so thankful that You know all about the future. Thank You for Your good plans. Amen.

GOOD WORK IS HARD WORK

So let's not get tired of doing what is good. At just the right time we will reap a harvest of blessing if we don't give up.

GALATIANS 6:9 NLT

Sometimes doing the right thing means saying yes—to helping out with chores or sharing what you have. Sometimes it means saying no—to selfishness and unkind words. It's not always easy to make the right choice. You might even get tired of doing what's good—especially if no one seems to pay attention! But don't give up! God sees you making good choices and He knows you're working hard. He loves to see you thinking about your words, helping a sibling, or spending your time with someone who feels left out. So keep going! God is cheering you on!

THOUGHT OF THE DAY

Are good choices ever hard for you? Talk to your parents! Maybe they have some ideas to help.

PRAY TODAY

Dear God, sometimes it's easier to make the wrong choice. Help me to be strong so I can choose good things all the time! Amen.

COUNT ON GOD'S GOODNESS

Surely goodness and mercy shall follow me all the days of my life, and I shall dwell in the house of the LORD forever.

PSALM 23:6 ESV

The Bible tells us that God is good. Does that mean that only good things happen to people? No. Sometimes bad things happen. People get sick. People get hurt. Things don't always turn out the way we would like.

But that doesn't mean that God is not good. God never leaves us. God always helps us, even when bad things happen. God comforts us. He sends friends and family to share His love with us. He can even bring good things out of bad times! You can always count on God, because He is always good!

THOUGHT OF THE DAY

What are some ways God has shown His goodness to you?

PRAY TODAY

Dear God, thank You for always being good. I'm so glad I can always count on Your love for me. Amen.

THANK YOU, GOD

Praise the LORD. Give thanks to the LORD, for he is good; his love endures forever.

PSALM 106:1 NIV

How do you feel when you give someone a present, but they don't say thanks? If you help someone, but they never even take time to thank you, how does it make you feel?

Think about all the wonderful gifts God gives you every day—family, friends, answered prayers, a home, and all of nature. You are God's beloved child, and He loves to give you good things. He also loves to know that you are thankful. Be sure to take time each day to give thanks to the Lord.

THOUGHT OF THE DAY

What are some things you want to thank God for today?

PRAY TODAY

Dear God, thank You for all Your amazing and good gifts. I love You. Amen.

LEARN TO LAUGH

He will yet fill your mouth with laughter, and your lips with shouting.

JOB 8:21 ESV

Bob and Larry love to tell jokes. Here's a good one: What was the only animal Noah couldn't trust to play fair? The cheetah! Here's another: Why couldn't they play card games on the ark? Because Noah was always standing on the deck!

Telling funny jokes and being silly is just fine with God. He loves to hear us laugh. Some people think that God wants us to be serious all the time. But that's not what the Bible says. When you're happy, laugh. When you feel silly, giggle. Let others know that "God has filled your mouth with laughter!"

THOUGHT OF THE DAY

What makes you laugh? Do you have a favorite VeggieTales silly song that you like to sing?

PRAY TODAY

Dear God, I love to laugh. Please help me bring joy to others too. Amen.

GOD'S SURPRISES

"Do you think you can explain the mystery of God? Do you think you can diagram God Almighty? God is far higher than you can imagine, far deeper than you can comprehend."

JOB 11:7–8 MSG

Has God ever surprised you? Maybe something wonderful happened that you weren't expecting! Or maybe you didn't get what you wanted. God's surprises can be exciting, disappointing, or just plain confusing! But never forget: God knows best. God loves you. And He has amazing plans for you!

When things don't happen the way you hoped, ask God to help you find and share joy in every situation. You may feel disappointed, but keep trusting God. His plans are even greater than you can imagine!

THOUGHT OF THE DAY

We can't understand everything about God. But we can understand that He loves us.

PRAY TODAY

Dear God, please help me remember that Your plan is best, even when it's not what I expected! Amen.

DON'T GIVE UP

Let us run with endurance the race that is set before us.

HEBREWS 12:1 ESV

If you're running a race, do you sit down before the finish line? When you're working on a model or a puzzle, do you stop halfway through?

To win a race or finish a project, you have to keep going! Life is like that too. There are many things to learn and do. Sometimes you might want to give up or quit. But the Bible tells us to keep on going, even when things are difficult or boring. After all, you'll never know the joy of finishing if you don't endure to the end!

THOUGHT OF THE DAY

When you feel like giving up, ask God to help you keep going.

PRAY TODAY

Dear God, help me remember that You are there to help me when I feel like giving up. Thank You. Amen.

REAL FAITH

In the same way, faith by itself, if it is not accompanied by action, is dead.

JAMES 2:17 NIV

I f someone says they are your friend, you expect them to act like a friend. If you say someone is your friend, they expect you to act like a friend too. We prove our friendship by what we do.

Faith is like that too. When we say we love and believe in God and His Son, Jesus, then our actions should prove it. How? By doing the things Jesus says to do. Tell the truth. Be kind. Treat others the way you want to be treated. We show that our faith is real through the things we do, not just the words we say.

THOUGHT OF THE DAY

What is something you can do today to prove your faith is real?

PRAY TODAY

Dear God, please help me act and speak in ways that show my faith is real. Amen.

RUN THE RIGHT WAY

Run from temptations that capture young people. Always do the right thing.

2 TIMOTHY 2:22A CEV

When you are tempted, you really, really want to do something you know you shouldn't. Whether it's sneaking an extra piece of candy or lying to get out of trouble, temptation can be hard to resist! So God says we should "run from temptation."

Sometimes that means actually leaving a place where you feel tempted—like walking away from the candy bowl or from friends who tell lies. You can also pray for courage to do the right thing, even when it's hard. Keep practicing good choices, and it'll get easier to turn down temptation.

THOUGHT OF THE DAY

When do you get tempted? Make a plan! How will you "run from temptation" next time?

PRAY TODAY

Dear God, sometimes I really want to do things I shouldn't do. Please help me run from temptation and do what's right! Amen.

CHOOSE WISDOM

Wisdom is more precious than rubies. Nothing you could want is equal to it.

PROVERBS 8:11 NCV

What's the best gift you've ever received? God told Solomon to ask for anything he wanted, and do you know what he asked for? Wisdom! Solomon knew that making wise choices was more important than being rich or popular. Because of God's great gift, Solomon became a king whose people loved and respected him.

You can ask God for wisdom too! God loves to help us make good decisions that show His love. When you're in a tough spot, ask God what He wants you to do. He can make you as wise as a king (or queen)!

THOUGHT OF THE DAY

Can you think of a time God helped you make a wise choice?

PRAY TODAY

Dear God, thank You for good gifts like wisdom! Remind me to check with You so my choices are the wisest ones. Amen.

YOU CAN TRUST GOD

Trust in the LORD with all your heart; do not depend on your own understanding.

PROVERBS 3:5 NLT

Sometimes when you're feeling sad or angry or frustrated, you can't imagine how things will get better. It seems impossible. That is when you need to trust God even more. Do you know why? Because God can do anything!

You might be smart or strong, but even the strongest person can't do the things God can do. He can heal your heart after someone has hurt your feelings. He can give you courage to apologize when you need to. He can give you new ideas about how to solve a problem. So when you are having a hard time, pray. Then trust God to do what you cannot.

THOUGHT OF THE DAY

God is greater than any of your problems!

PRAY TODAY

Dear God, when I can't see a way to make things better, please help me to trust You more. Amen.

WANT OR NEED

"So don't worry at all about having enough food and clothing. . . . But your heavenly Father already knows perfectly well that you need them, and he will give them to you if you give him first place in your life and live as he wants you to."

MATTHEW 6:31–33 TLB

God knows everything about you. He knows your favorite color, your best friend, and your biggest dreams. He knows everything you want! But more importantly, He knows exactly what you need.

When you put God first, He promises to give you the things you need to live the life He's planned for you. So don't worry about having the newest books or the biggest toys. Instead, try to follow God the very best you can. God knows what you need, and He will always take care of you!

THOUGHT OF THE DAY

Think of something you want and something you need. How are they different?

PRAY TODAY

Dear God, help me remember that You will give me everything I need. Amen.

GOD'S PLANS FOR YOU

"The LORD who saved me from a lion and a bear will save me from this Philistine."

1 SAMUEL 17:37A NCV

David was a famous warrior and king. But he didn't start out that way. When David was young, he spent his days alone, taking care of smelly sheep! It was a dirty, boring, and sometimes scary job.

But God knew something David didn't. God knew that one day David would need the skills he used to protect his sheep to become a brave king who could protect God's people. God knows your future too, and He can use what you are learning now to help you become the person He wants you to be! God has exciting plans for you!

THOUGHT OF THE DAY

Grow and learn all that you can, so you can do what God has planned!

PRAY TODAY

Dear God, I don't know what You have planned for me, but You do. Help me get ready! Amen.

KEEP ON BURNING!

Don't burn out; keep yourselves fueled and aflame. Be alert servants of the Master, cheerfully expectant. Don't quit in hard times; pray all the harder.

ROMANS 12:11–12 MSG

A fire can keep you warm on a cold night or light up a dark room. God says that we should be like a warm, bright fire! Then we can help others feel God's comfort and shine a light to show them how to follow Him. And just like a fire needs wood to keep on burning, you need fuel to stay strong!

What kind of fuel does a person need? Healthy food helps your body grow. Spending time with friends and family helps you love others well. And plenty of time with God will keep you joyful and courageous. So fuel up! Then you'll be ready for anything.

THOUGHT OF THE DAY

Don't run out of fuel. Make time for God every day!

PRAY TODAY

Dear God, thank You for being my fuel! Help me keep on burning for You every day. Amen.

WHAT DO YOU TRUST?

"But blessed are those who trust in the LORD and have made the LORD their hope and confidence."

JEREMIAH 17:7 NLT

People put their trust in all kinds of different things. Some people trust in their brains or their muscles. Some people trust in the things they own or being popular. When you trust in something, you are counting on it to always be there for you.

But guess what? Brains, muscles, what you own, and popularity can all change. Trusting in something that can change is risky. But do you know what never changes? God! And God says if you trust in Him you will always have blessings. God will always be there for you!

THOUGHT OF THE DAY

Why can you always trust in God?

PRAY TODAY

Dear God, thank You for being trustworthy. I am so glad I can always count on You. Amen.

HONOR YOUR PARENTS

"Honor your father and mother. Then you will live a long, full life in the land the Lᴏʀᴅ your God is giving you."

EXODUS 20:12 NLT

The Ten Commandments are God's rules for living a good life. They are all important, but did you know that there is only one with a promise? It's the fifth commandment. Read the verse above and see if you can find the promise.

Honoring your parents can mean doing what they ask without whining or talking back. It can also mean following their rules, helping them, and showing them you are grateful for all they do. God gives you parents so you can know how it feels to be loved. Loving them back is a way you can obey God and live a full, happy life together.

THOUGHT OF THE DAY

What are some ways you honor your parents?

PRAY TODAY

Dear God, thank You for my parents. Please help me to honor them, so they know how much I love them, and we can all be happy together. Amen.

HEARING EARS

"He who has ears to hear, let him hear."

MATTHEW 11:15 ESV

Do you know that you can hear something without really listening to it? Does you mom or dad ever say, "I just told you that!" Or maybe you heard a friend talking, but you don't remember what she said, because you weren't really listening.

Often, when Jesus told a story, He said: "He who has ears to hear, let him hear." What He meant was: Listen to what I'm saying and understand it. When you read the Bible, take time to hear and listen to what God is telling you. Pay attention. Then do what Jesus says.

THOUGHT OF THE DAY

Hear not only with your ears, but also with your mind.

PRAY TODAY

Dear God, I want to follow You. Please help me really listen to Your words. Amen.

P.R.A.Y.

"Pray like this: Our Father in heaven, may your name be kept holy. May your Kingdom come soon. May your will be done on earth as it is in heaven."

MATTHEW 6:9-10 NLT

Prayer is a way of talking to God. Sometimes we say prayers that we have memorized, and other times we just make up prayers. If you have trouble thinking about how to pray, here is a helpful trick. Just use the letters in the word PRAY!

P = Praise God for who He is and what He has done.

R = Repent. Ask God to forgive you for doing what you shouldn't or not doing what you should.

A = Ask God to help others.

Y = Ask God to help YOU.

Remember that you can always talk to God, and He will always hear you!

THOUGHT OF THE DAY

When do you enjoy praying?

PRAY TODAY

Dear God, thank You for always listening to me when I pray. Help me learn to listen to You too! Amen.

GOD CAN DO ANYTHING

Jesus looked at them and said, "With man this is impossible, but with God all things are possible."

MATTHEW 19:26 NIV

D o you sometimes feel like you aren't good enough? Maybe you try and try to keep from saying unkind things, but sometimes you do anyway. Maybe you really want to tell the truth, but sometimes you don't.

God knows that even though we want to do what's right, we often fail. But Jesus tells us that when we can't do what we want, He is there to help us. He can do anything! Nothing is impossible for God. Next time you want to do the right thing, ask God to help you. With God, all things are possible!

THOUGHT OF THE DAY
When we are weak, Jesus is strong!

PRAY TODAY
Dear God, I'm so glad that You are always there. Please help me remember to ask You when I need help.

@ @ @ @ @ @ @ @

LOYAL FRIENDS

But Ruth said, "Do not urge me to leave you or to return from following you. For where you go I will go, and where you lodge I will lodge. Your people shall be my people, and your God my God."

RUTH 1:16 ESV

Good friends are so important. You enjoy playing, talking, and spending time together! But another quality that makes someone a good friend is loyalty. Loyalty means you are honest and trustworthy, and you stand up for your friend in good times and bad times.

It's easy to stay friends with someone who is happy all the time. But what do you do when a friend is sad or going through some hard times? If you are loyal, you always look for ways to encourage and support your friend. Loyal friends are there for each other!

THOUGHT OF THE DAY

Who has been a loyal friend to you? How are you loyal to your friends?

PRAY TODAY

Dear God, thank You for loyal friends. Please help me to be a true and loyal friend too. Amen.

POWER IN PRAISE

I will bless the LORD at all times; His praise shall continually be in my mouth.

PSALM 34:1 AMP

Some people wonder why they should praise God. They think, "God already knows how great He is, so why should I tell Him?" But here's the most important thing about praise: Praise reminds us how great God is! When we talk about the amazing things God does or sing about His goodness, we remember that He is more powerful than any fears or doubts we might feel.

God knows we often feel small or afraid. That's why He wants us to praise Him! As we speak of His greatness, power, and love, our bad feelings disappear!

THOUGHT OF THE DAY

Praising God builds our faith.

PRAY TODAY

Dear God, You are so great! Nothing can ever take Your love from me. Thank You. Amen.

@ @ @ @ @ @ @ @

HOW TO TREAT OTHERS

"Treat others just as you want to be treated."

LUKE 6:31 CEV

When someone has a toy you want, do you grab it? If someone gives you a gift, do you take it and never say thank you? At the dinner table, do you yell, "Hey, where's my food?" Even Mr. Nezzer knows that's not how to act!

Saying please and thank you shows respect for others. Asking politely and being grateful for what we have is just good manners. The Bible says to treat others the way we want to be treated. When we do, we are following Jesus' example.

THOUGHT OF THE DAY

Think about how you like to be treated, then treat others the same way!

PRAY TODAY

Dear God, please help me to remember to be thoughtful and kind. Amen.

A CHILD OF THE KING

And if children, then heirs—heirs of God and fellow heirs with Christ.

ROMANS 8:17A ESV

An heir is a child who has a right to what his or her parents own. The Bible says you are an heir of God. That means you are a part of God's family, and you can have all the wonderful things God has prepared for His children!

When you love Jesus and trust in Him, God gives you amazing gifts! He gives you love, peace, and joy. He gives you power and strength to overcome problems. When you belong to God's family, you are a princess because you are a child of the King!

THOUGHT OF THE DAY

You are precious to God, because you are His child!

PRAY TODAY

Dear God, I am so glad You chose me to be Your child. Thank You for loving me so much. Amen.

GOD ALWAYS LISTENS

Rejoice always! Pray constantly. Give thanks in everything, for this is God's will for you in Christ Jesus.

1 THESSALONIANS 5:16-18 HCSB

Sometimes we think about prayer as asking God for things. But prayer is much more than just asking. If you have a good friend, don't you love to tell them about all the fun and exciting things that are going on? Jesus wants to hear about those things too!

You can talk to Jesus out loud or in your mind. Tell Him about what makes you happy. Talk to Him about the things you are thankful for. When you spend time sharing joyful and grateful moments with Jesus, you will find it easy to pray.

THOUGHT OF THE DAY

What are some things you want to tell Jesus today?

PRAY TODAY

Dear God, I'm so glad You are always there. Thank You for listening to me. Amen.

A SPECIAL GIFT

You must encourage one another each day.

HEBREWS 3:13A CEV

There's a special gift you can give that doesn't cost anything. You don't have to wrap it up. And it doesn't even take up any space in your pocket. Do you know what it is? Encouragement!

Encouragement can be as simple as saying "hi" to someone who is feeling lonely. Or listening to a friend who is feeling sad. You can encourage someone with a hug or a smile. You can ask him to play with you or help her learn something new. Everyone needs encouragement. And here's a secret surprise: When you encourage someone else, the gift often comes back to you!

THOUGHT OF THE DAY
How will you encourage someone today?

PRAY TODAY
Dear God, please show me how to encourage others each day. Then help me to do it! Amen.

BE COURAGEOUS

"Be strong! Be courageous! Do not be afraid of them! For the Lord your God will be with you. He will neither fail you nor forsake you."

DEUTERONOMY 31:6 TLB

When you hear the word "courage" what do you think about? Superheroes who fight evil villains? Explorers who face wild animals?

Those aren't the only ways to be courageous. Courage is standing up for someone who is being teased or bullied. It is facing your fears of speaking up in class or trying something new. It is trying again and again when you make mistakes.

Here's some good news: the Bible says that when you need courage, you can count always on God to be with you. So be courageous!

THOUGHT OF THE DAY

When was a time you needed to be courageous?

PRAY TODAY

Dear God, I'm so glad that when I feel nervous or afraid I can always count on You to give me courage! Amen.

THE SECRET TO JOY

"You will live in joy and peace."

ISAIAH 55:12A NLT

Joy is a little word, but it makes a big difference in your life. And here's a secret for finding joy. Use the letters in the word to remember what brings real joy: J is for putting Jesus first. O is for showing His love to others. Y is for loving yourself too! J+O+Y=JOY

If you remember this little formula, your life will be filled with joy and peace. When you love Jesus and share His love with others, you will discover that your heart fills up with good things. That's how to live the way God wants you to!

THOUGHT OF THE DAY

Living as God wants you to—it's Jesus, then others, then you!

PRAY TODAY

Dear God, please help me find real joy by putting You first. Amen.

TRUST GOD

Commit everything you do to the LORD. Trust him, and he will help you.

PSALM 37:5 NLT

God says that we can always trust Him. That means when God makes a promise, He keeps it.

And one of the best promises He's made is to help His children—with everything! Have you ever felt scared? Ask God to take away your fear. Are you learning something new? Pray for the patience to keep trying. Are you lonely? Ask Him to bring good friends your way! Talk to God anytime, about anything. When you trust God, He can help you. It's what He loves to do!

THOUGHT OF THE DAY

How do you know God loves you? Did He say it? Then it's true!

PRAY TODAY

Dear God, I'm so glad I can trust You. Help me remember to ask for Your help when I am having a hard time. Amen.

JESUS LOVES YOU!

"You're blessed when you're content with just who you are—no more, no less."

MATTHEW 5:5A MSG

God loves everything about you. No one else does things exactly like you do them or has exactly your ideas. No one else can love your family and friends like you can. The world needs you! You're amazing!

But you might not always feel amazing. You might wish you looked different, or thought differently, or were more like someone else. When you start feeling that way, remember that Jesus loves you right now. Not you with different hair or a quieter voice or more friends or bigger toys. He loves you just as you are. And you should love you too!

THOUGHT OF THE DAY

What are three things you love about yourself?

PRAY TODAY

Dear God, I am Your special creation. Thank You for making me just the way I am. Amen.

GOD'S SPECIAL LANGUAGE

"My sheep hear My voice, I know them, and they follow Me."

JOHN 10:27 HCSB

Have you ever noticed grown-ups talking about "hearing God's voice"? That's a little confusing, because most of the time, we don't hear God like we hear other people! Instead, God uses other ways to talk to us.

God likes to give us good thoughts that are hard to ignore. Do you have a great idea for helping others? Do you find that you can't stop thinking about inviting the new kid to play or apologizing for a mistake you made? Sometimes God speaks by giving us courage when we need to do something hard or scary. Pay attention to God's special language. When you do, you'll "hear" great things!

THOUGHT OF THE DAY

You hear God best when you listen with your heart.

PRAY TODAY

Dear God, I want to hear Your voice. Help me pay attention with my heart so I'll always know what You're saying! Amen.

HOW WOULD YOU LIKE IT?

"Just as you want others to do for you, do the same for them."

LUKE 6:31 HCSB

The Bible says we should treat others the way we'd like to be treated. So let's play a game. Imagine you're playing with two friends—one uses good manners and the other uses no manners at all. Which one would let you go first or say "I'm sorry" if she made a mistake? Who might push or hit to get what he wants? What kinds of words would each friend say if he or she didn't get his or her way? And which friend would you like to play with again tomorrow?

Next time you're with friends, remember the two pretend ones you imagined today. Then act like the friend you'd like to have!

THOUGHT OF THE DAY

Use good manners—you can't go wrong!
You'll show kindness all day long.

PRAY TODAY

Dear God, please help me remember good manners so I will always treat others with kindness. Amen.

A GREAT BIG FAMILY

"And I will be a father to you, and you shall be sons and daughters to me, says the Lord Almighty."

2 CORINTHIANS 6:18 ESV

A loving family is one of God's greatest gifts. When the people in a family care for and support each other, home feels like the safest, happiest place in the world.

And guess what? We are all part of God's family! He's our loving parent, cheering us on, holding us when we're scared, and helping us learn and grow every day.

Do you know someone who doesn't have a happy family? Look for ways to be a loving sister to them. Then they can feel happily at home as part of God's great big family!

THOUGHT OF THE DAY

Who lives at your house? Is your family big or small?

PRAY TODAY

Dear God, thank You for the gift of my family! Help me act like a good sister to others. Amen.

GOD'S GOT THIS

Since God assured us, "I'll never let you down, never walk off and leave you," we can boldly quote, "God is there, ready to help; I'm fearless no matter what. Who or what can get to me?"

HEBREWS 13:5-6 MSG

Did you know that God is the answer to every problem? No matter what you're facing, God can help. Sometimes just talking to God can help you feel better. Praying for courage or peace is a great way to overcome fears! God often works through people and will provide helpers like parents or friends to guide you. And other times, God will give you an idea for a solution to try! There are so many different ways He can help us. But one thing's always true: nothing is too hard for God!

THOUGHT OF THE DAY

Is there something you need help with today? Talk to God about it!

PRAY TODAY

Dear God, please help me when I feel discouraged. I'm so glad nothing is too hard for You. Amen.

SPEAK GENTLY

Always be humble, gentle, and patient, accepting each other in love.

EPHESIANS 4:2 NCV

Do you ever have a hard time being quiet? Maybe you love to talk first—or loudest—to make sure everyone hears you. And when you have something interesting to say, it's hard to wait your turn!

The Bible tells us to be gentle with each other. You probably know to be gentle with your actions, but it's important that your words are gentle too. Speaking gently means you choose kind, helpful words. It means being patient when others are speaking and paying attention too. When you listen carefully, you can respond with wisdom, care, and your own great ideas!

THOUGHT OF THE DAY

Words can be as powerful as actions—use both gently!

PRAY TODAY

Dear God, thank You for giving me good ideas. Please help me be patient, pay attention, and then use my words to help! Amen.

TALK ABOUT IT

"Those who are sad now are happy. God will comfort them."

MATTHEW 5:4 ICB

No one can be happy all day every day. We all feel sad sometimes, and that's OK!

But don't be sad all by yourself. Talk to someone! God cares about your feelings, and He's given you loving people who are ready to listen. Your parents know you best, and maybe they've felt some of the same feelings you have. A good friend can also listen and encourage you. Teachers, grandparents, and siblings can be great listeners too. And don't forget that you can talk to God anytime you want to. In fact, He's the best place to start!

THOUGHT OF THE DAY

Happy or sad, you are never alone. God loves you!

PRAY TODAY

Dear God, please help me remember to talk to You when I'm sad. Then help me talk to others who love me too. Amen.

BELIEVE IN YOURSELF

"Don't be afraid. Only believe."

MARK 5:36B HCSB

Can you think of a time you tried something new? Sometimes new things feel scary. But when you trust Jesus, you don't need to be afraid. And in today's verse, Jesus even gives you the secret to trusting Him: just believe!

When you feel nervous to try something new, remember and believe the things Jesus says: He loves you, He'll never leave you, and He's given you good gifts. Then jump in and do your best! You won't do things perfectly at first—no one does! Just remind yourself of Jesus' promises, learn from your mistakes, and try again. Your next new thing might become your new favorite thing!

THOUGHT OF THE DAY

Is there something new you want to try? Ask Jesus to help you learn!

PRAY TODAY

Dear Jesus, I believe that You are always with me. Please give me courage and patience to try new things! Amen.

FOLLOW YOUR HEART

Finally, all of you should be of one mind. Sympathize with each other. Love each other as brothers and sisters. Be tenderhearted, and keep a humble attitude.

1 PETER 3:8 NLT

Think of someone you love. How do you like to treat them? Most of us are kind to the people we love. And that's good!

But God wants us to show kindness to everyone— including those we don't know or even get along with! That's a little harder, but here's a trick: check with your heart! Do you have a feeling inside that you should invite a new neighbor to your birthday party? Or stop sharing gossip? Or donate some of your allowance to help hungry people eat? That's your heart helping you find kindness. So follow your heart! Kindness is always the best choice.

THOUGHT OF THE DAY

Kindness starts in your heart—but it doesn't stop there!

PRAY TODAY

Dear God, please show me how to be kind to everyone! Amen.

BLOW YOUR WORRIES AWAY!

Give all your worries and cares to God, for he cares about you.

1 PETER 5:7 NLT

Have you ever felt worried? Worry happens when you can't stop thinking about a problem. God doesn't want you to spend all your energy worrying about things. Instead, He says to give your worries to Him!

How can you do that? A fun way to picture it is by blowing bubbles. Imagine that each bubble has a worry inside it. Then, watch them float up, up, and away. Ask God to take each worry and get rid of it. As the bubbles pop or disappear into the sky, thank God for lifting your worries from your mind.

THOUGHT OF THE DAY

Fill your mind with God each day. He can carry your cares away!

PRAY TODAY

Dear God, thank You for caring about me. Please take my worries away! Amen.

BIG PROMISES

"But your name shall be Abraham, for I have made you the father of a multitude of nations."

GENESIS 17:5 ESV

God has always loved to surprise us. A long time ago, He made a big promise to a man named Abraham. God told Abraham that one day his family would be so big it would stretch across the whole world. But here was the problem: Abraham had no children. And most people thought he and his wife were too old to start a family. But they had faith—which means they believed God, even when it seemed impossible. And God kept His promise! Abraham and Sarah had a son, and today their descendants fill the world. God can do anything!

THOUGHT OF THE DAY

Can you think of some other promises God made to people in the Bible?

PRAY TODAY

Dear God, I love Your surprises! Help me remember to have faith in You, even when the things You promise seem impossible.

REAL PEACE

"I leave you peace. My peace I give you. I do not give it to you as the world does. So don't let your hearts be troubled."

JOHN 14:27 ICB

D o you know what peace is? It's a feeling of calmness and being sure that everything will be OK. But there are two kinds of peace: the kind that goes away when things get tough, and the kind that sticks around no matter that. The second kind is real peace, and that's what God promises to give you.

When things go wrong, or you feel angry, sad, or afraid, ask God to give you His gift of real peace. The things around you may not change, but God will change your heart. He'll help you find peace anywhere.

THOUGHT OF THE DAY

How do you think it feels to be peaceful?

PRAY TODAY

Dear God, when I feel upset, help me remember to ask for Your gift of peace. Amen.

OVER AND OVER AGAIN

"Rebuke your brother if he sins, and forgive him if he is sorry. Even if he wrongs you seven times a day and each time turns again and asks forgiveness, forgive him."

LUKE 17:3-4 TLB

There are no limits on God's forgiveness. He will always welcome us back into His arms and let us try again, over and over. Doesn't that feel great?

God says that we should forgive others in the same way. It's not easy! You might not feel like forgiving a classmate who hurts your feelings or a sister who ruins your art project. Especially if it keeps happening. But God doesn't want you to limit your forgiveness. So ask for His help. He can give you the strength and courage to forgive others over and over again.

THOUGHT OF THE DAY

How does it feel to be forgiven?

PRAY TODAY

Dear God, it isn't always easy to forgive, but I can do it with Your help. Help me forgive over and over, just like You do. Amen.

SEVENTY TIMES SEVEN

Then Peter came to him and asked, "Lord, how often should I forgive someone who sins against me? Seven times?" "No, not seven times," Jesus replied, "but seventy times seven!"

MATTHEW 18:21-22 NLT

Forgiveness isn't always easy. True forgiveness means we let go of wanting to get back at the person who hurt us. That's important, because God doesn't want feelings of anger to keep growing inside you. But it doesn't always happen right away.

So what if you try to forgive someone but that feeling doesn't go away? Should you give up? No! God says you should try until you get it right! You don't have to do it alone. Ask God for His help to forgive others the right way. Then keep trying. When true forgiveness happens, you'll feel so much better!

THOUGHT OF THE DAY
Forgiveness is good for everyone!

PRAY TODAY
Dear God, please help me forgive the right way—even if it takes a few tries! Amen.

THE GIFT OF LOVE

"For this is how God loved the world: He gave his one and only Son, so that everyone who believes in him will not perish but have eternal life."

JOHN 3:16 NLT

Sometimes we show our love for others by giving gifts. You might pick a big bouquet of flowers for your parents or spend your allowance to buy the perfect birthday present for your best friend. When you love someone, you want them to know!

God loves us so much, so He sent the most wonderful gift: Jesus. Jesus showed us what God's goodness looks like. He healed the sick, cared for the lonely, and invited everyone to be in God's family. Then He died and rose again so that we can all live in heaven with Him forever. What amazing love!

THOUGHT OF THE DAY

When you say a prayer of praise, it's like giving a gift back to God!

PRAY TODAY

Dear God, thank You for the wonderful gift of Jesus and for loving me so much! Amen.

LEADERS NEED PRAYERS TOO!

Pray for rulers and for all who have authority so that we can have quiet and peaceful lives full of worship and respect for God.

1 TIMOTHY 2:2 NCV

Who are some leaders you know about? You might think about someone famous, like a king or a president, but there are lots of leaders right in your community too. What about teachers, pastors, counselors, and parents? Every leader makes important decisions that affect others. So they all need God's guidance and wisdom! And you can make a difference by praying for your leaders. Ask God to help each one be honest, kind, and wise. Pray for peace and fairness everywhere. When you pray for powerful people, God can do powerful things!

THOUGHT OF THE DAY

Would you like to be a leader someday? What kind of leader would you be?

PRAY TODAY

Dear God, sometimes I forget that powerful people need prayers too. Please let those who lead us know Your wisdom and love. Amen.

CARING THROUGH SHARING

Give generously, for your gifts will return to you later.

ECCLESIASTES 11:1 TLB

Being generous means sharing what you have with others, even when it's hard. Sometimes that looks like giving away the money in your piggy bank to help feed people who can't buy food. Other times, it's donating old toys and books to your church or even splitting your snack in half to share with a friend who forgot hers. You might not always feel like being generous, but once you try it, it feels pretty great. In fact, it can be fun! See if you can find new ways to be generous each day. God promises to bless you for caring through sharing.

THOUGHT OF THE DAY

Can you think of a time when someone was generous to you?

PRAY TODAY

Dear God, it's fun to make others happy! Help me to be generous with all the blessings You've given me. Amen.

YOU CAN TRUST HIM

"Do not be afraid or discouraged. For the LORD your God is with you wherever you go."

JOSHUA 1:9B NLT

Have you ever made a promise you couldn't keep? Has anyone ever broken a promise to you? When a promise is broken, it can be hard to trust that person again.

But do you know who never breaks a promise? God. And that's great news, because His promises are amazing! He says that He will give you rest. He'll be with you wherever you go. Nothing can separate you from His love. And through Jesus, He's promised you eternal life. You can feel good about trusting God. He always tells the truth, and He always keeps His promises.

THOUGHT OF THE DAY

God's promises are always true. Trusting Him is the thing to do!

PRAY TODAY

Dear God, thank You for keeping all Your wonderful promises. I'm glad I can trust You! Amen.

LAST OR FIRST

"So you want first place? Then take the last place. Be the servant of all."

MARK 9:35 MSG

When most people think about being first, they think about feeling like the most important person in the room. Maybe they get there by winning a trophy or having the most toys or being the line leader. But according to Jesus, none of that matters. Instead, to be first in God's kingdom, He says we should put ourselves last. That means helping and encouraging others, even if it slows us down or allows someone else to get more attention. When you do that, you make God smile. And that's the only first place prize that matters!

THOUGHT OF THE DAY

Can you find a way to put someone else first today?

PRAY TODAY

Dear God, I like being first. Please help me remember that to be first in Your eyes, I need to put myself last. Amen.

HIS VERY OWN

Long ago, even before he made the world, God chose us to be his very own through what Christ would do for us. . . . And he did this because he wanted to!

EPHESIANS 1:4-5 TLB

God loves you. You might already know that, but did you know that He loved you even before you were born? The Bible says God loved you even before the world began! He knew who you would be, and He wanted you to be part of His family. You are important to God.

You might feel upset or frustrated sometimes. Maybe you even wish you could change certain things about yourself. But God loves you just the way you are. He chose you to be His very own, and He'll never change His mind.

THOUGHT OF THE DAY

God chose you—so you are wonderful!

PRAY TODAY

Dear God, Your love makes me so happy! Thank You! Amen.

MAKE GOOD CHOICES

Finally, brothers, whatever is true, whatever is honorable, whatever is just, whatever is pure, whatever is lovely, whatever is commendable, if there is any excellence, if there is anything worthy of praise, think about these things.

PHILIPPIANS 4:8 ESV

What kind of books and movies do you like? What do you talk about with your friends? The Bible says the things you think about can shape your attitudes and feelings. Some books and movies help us enjoy life and encourage us to help others. But some can make us feel worried or angry. We can talk with friends in kind ways, or we can gossip and spread rumors. It's up to you! God wants us to make choices that will lead to good attitudes. So ask Him to help you spend your time—and thoughts—wisely!

THOUGHT OF THE DAY

Reading Bible stories each day is a great way to fill your thoughts with good things!

PRAY TODAY

Dear God, please help me spend time on things that will make me happy and kind. Amen.

WHAT A FRIEND!

"Just as the Father has loved Me, I also have loved you; remain in My love."

JOHN 15:9 HCSB

There's an old song that says, "What a friend we have in Jesus!" Do you know what makes Jesus such a good friend? He always wants the best for you, and He loves you, no matter what.

Jesus doesn't compare you to anyone else. He wants you to do the things God made you to do, and He encourages you along the way. He'll always listen to you and help you when you ask.

So don't forget to spend time in prayer each day. Hanging out with Jesus will make your friendship even stronger!

THOUGHT OF THE DAY

What do you talk about with your friends? Share those things with Jesus too!

PRAY TODAY

Dear Jesus, You are such a great friend! Help me remember to spend time with You every day! Amen.

MOM OR DAD, HELP YOUR DAUGHTER MEMORIZE THIS VERSE
AND TALK TO HER ABOUT WHAT IT MEANS.

"I have told you these things
so you may have peace in Me.
In the world you will have much trouble.
But take hope!
I have power over the world!"

—

JOHN 16:33 NLV

MOM OR DAD, HELP YOUR DAUGHTER MEMORIZE THIS VERSE
AND TALK TO HER ABOUT WHAT IT MEANS.

No matter what happens,
always be thankful,
for this is God's will for you
who belong to Christ Jesus.

—

1 THESSALONIANS 5:18 TLB

KNOW IT BY HEART

MOM OR DAD, HELP YOUR DAUGHTER MEMORIZE THIS VERSE
AND TALK TO HER ABOUT WHAT IT MEANS.

We love because God first loved us.

—

1 JOHN 4:19 ICB

MOM OR DAD, HELP YOUR DAUGHTER MEMORIZE THIS VERSE
AND TALK TO HER ABOUT WHAT IT MEANS.

"The LORD does not look at
the things people look at.
People look at the outward appearance,
but the LORD looks at the heart."

—

1 SAMUEL 16:7B NIV

MOM OR DAD, HELP YOUR DAUGHTER MEMORIZE THIS VERSE
AND TALK TO HER ABOUT WHAT IT MEANS.

"In the same way, let your good deeds
shine out for all to see,
so that everyone will praise
your heavenly Father."

—

MATTHEW 5:16 NLT

MOM OR DAD, HELP YOUR DAUGHTER MEMORIZE THIS VERSE
AND TALK TO HER ABOUT WHAT IT MEANS.

Your word is a lamp to my feet
And a light to my path.

—

PSALM 119:105 AMP

MOM OR DAD, HELP YOUR DAUGHTER MEMORIZE THIS VERSE
AND TALK TO HER ABOUT WHAT IT MEANS.

If you do not have wisdom, ask God for it.
He is always ready to give it to you
and will never say you are
wrong for asking.

—

JAMES 1:5 NLV

MOM OR DAD, HELP YOUR DAUGHTER MEMORIZE THIS VERSE
AND TALK TO HER ABOUT WHAT IT MEANS.

"Be strong and brave. Don't be afraid
of them and don't be frightened,
because the LORD your God
will go with you.
He will not leave you or forget you."

—

DEUTERONOMY 31:6 NCV

KNOW IT BY HEART

MOM OR DAD, HELP YOUR DAUGHTER MEMORIZE THIS VERSE
AND TALK TO HER ABOUT WHAT IT MEANS.

This is what God commands:
that we believe in his Son, Jesus Christ,
and that we love each other,
just as he commanded.

—

1 JOHN 3:23 NCV

KNOW IT BY HEART

MOM OR DAD, HELP YOUR DAUGHTER MEMORIZE THIS VERSE
AND TALK TO HER ABOUT WHAT IT MEANS.

I will praise You because I have been
remarkably and wonderfully made.

—

PSALM 139:14 HCSB

KNOW IT BY HEART

MOM OR DAD, HELP YOUR DAUGHTER MEMORIZE THIS VERSE
AND TALK TO HER ABOUT WHAT IT MEANS.

Jesus said to him, "I am the way,
and the truth, and the life.
No one comes to the Father
except through me."

—

JOHN 14:6 ESV